REACHING THE AFFECT

REACHING THE AFFECT

Style in the Psychodynamic Therapies

EMANUEL HAMMER, PH.D.

Jason Aronson Inc.
Northvale, New Jersey
London

Library of Congress Cataloging-in-Publication Data

Hammer, Emanuel F. (Emanuel Frederick)
    Reaching the affect : style in the psychodynamic therapies /
Emanuel F. Hammer.
        p.   cm.
    Includes bibliographical references.
    ISBN 0-87668-818-0
    1. Psychotherapy—Technique.   2. Psycholinguistics.   I. Title.
RC489.P73H36   1989
616.89'14—dc20   89-38897
                                                                          CIP

Manufactured in the United States of America. Jason Aronson Inc. offers books and
cassettes. For information and catalog write to Jason Aronson Inc., 230 Livingston
Street, Northvale, New Jersey 07647.

For
Lila, Diane, and Cary

Contents

3

Fundamentals of Style   33

4

Poetic Style: Use of Imagery   47

5

Earthy Style   63

6

Creative Style   87

9

Confrontational Style   159

10

Psychoanalysis and the Literary Arts   179

References   191

Preface

Psychotherapy attempts to alleviate human distress. Relating is central to how we heal, and communicating is the tool we use in the service of this healing. In therapy, anything that interferes with communication and relating is explored and confronted. This book focuses on the shaping of communication in psychotherapy so that the therapist can more effectively reach through to the patient's zones of affect, the nodes of feelings that must be touched if anything meaningful is to occur. The book examines means to add to our more conventional interventive modalities the use of an appeal to the system of the sensibilities we call imagination. Here we address techniques to reach more vividly the mind's eye, the mind's ear, the mind's very membrane. And yet more, to connect where feelings pulse.

The book offers a practical approach to an inspiring challenge: that of elevating technique from mere craft to clinical art. For example, an illustrator is a craftsman, Van Gogh an artist. The therapist rises to artist when he knows how to break from a pedestrian conformity to the strictures of theory or method to liberate improvisation, intuitive hunches, imagination, and his/her creative capacities. The book explores styles of intervening, the *how* and *why* and *when* we might employ more artful interventions in an effort to help patients find a way to their feelings.[1]

When I read novels or poetry, or attend the theater,

---

[1]Research (Davison 1980, Gendlin 1981, Greenberg and Safran 1989, Luborsky et al. 1971, Wexler 1974) supports the clinically derived wisdom regarding the importance of getting patients *in touch with their feelings*. These studies find this factor central to a successful treatment outcome — perhaps *the* crucial element in making psychotherapy a vital, potent process of change. It is, after all, the precondition, the required soil in which the other treatment ingredients may take root. Without it, the other factors evaporate into inconsequentiality. Transference remains thin. Interpretations are mere academic exercises. The entire process feels sterile, toneless, hollow.

In their comprehensive review, Greenberg and Safran (1989) note that reaching one's affect facilitates adaptation and assists problem solving; without conscious affective texture "people feel empty, confused, and often fragmented," and they lack "the impetus from the action tendencies to motivate action" (p. 720).

Patients, too, add confirmation. They are often aware that in entering psychotherapy, as one patient of mine put it, "Sooner or later I know that what I'm going to have to confront here is my feelings." This is repeatedly demonstrated as the process goes along. It requires digging down through resisting layers of conflicted feelings to a network of emotions. There one can stand and hold up one's affect, along with one's past and one's present, to the light of understanding.

I am struck by the overlap between the creative arts and the process of the dynamic psychotherapies. This book builds an explicit bridge between them. In doing so I borrow from the arts (1) to reshape our techniques, (2) to move the therapeutic process toward greater richness, and (3) to achieve a more robust and fruitful professional identity in finding closer cousins in the novelist, playwright, and poet than in the physician (whether or not we have come to the practice of the analytic therapies via the medical-school route). The medical model, after its extended trial, has proved constricting.

Since, without fully realizing it, we keep more natural and more heuristic company with the arts than with the other adjacent fields, we may look to encourage a flow from the arts to our territory. For me, this attitude enlivens and enriches my work, and makes it less the "impossible profession."

In addition to learning from the master analysts, from our colleagues, and from our patients, it is to the arts that we might turn to study craft and style, to the philosophers to study the broader truths, and to the novelists, poets, and playwrights to study interpersonal subtleties and effective methods of expression. We can learn here the difference between a vigorous communication and one that sags with stodginess, the difference between live phrases and their stale, gray ashes.

This book is about therapy from the psychodynamic perspective. And it is about language. It is about the special shaping of language to improve technique, quicken the pace of treatment, and maximize change and growth.

Along the way we will discuss affirmative aspects of the therapeutic experience: humor, playfulness, metaphor, creativity, liberating the libido, celebrating the impulses, and a concept of expanded goals.

One central stream that joined into the flow that became this book is an interest in the visual and in the use of imagery in the therapist's interpretive style. Where did this work begin? Perhaps in childhood in the hours spent cartooning and drawing. In adolescence this affinity for the visual broadened to an interest in art and literature, surfacing in later years in my psychodiagnostic work when I became intrigued with how personality is expressed in the creative process. This led to research and publications on both creativity and projective drawings.[2] I discovered how much the poet, dual master of the visual (through use of metaphor) and the verbal, could teach the therapist about pithy and emotionally hued ways to communicate interpretations to patients. The experimentation, the sheer adventure of it, was begun in my *The Use of Interpretation in Treatment* (1968; now out of print) and is sorted out and further developed here.

The heart of the current book beats in chapters 4 and 5 on "Poetic Style" and "Earthy Style," for they treat the use of imagery and metaphor by the analyst as a specifically honed means of connecting with the patient's affect. Chapter 6 on "Creative Style" shows how this is facilitated. The work's second contribution is presented in chapters 8 and 9, where consideration is given to the analyst adjusting his style to gain maximum effect with patients of differing diagnostic integrations, and how this might be done with each. "Playful Style," chapter 7,

---

[2]This culminated, in the former domain, in *Creativity* (1961) and *Creativity, Talent and Personality* (1984), and in the latter area, in *The Clinical Application of Projective Drawings* (1958).

brings technique and theory of technique together as we discuss the expansion of our customary therapeutic goals and the concept of a fuller and healthier personality. Chapter 10 contains its beautiful passages from novelists and poets who bridge the literary arts and psychoanalysis.

When we compare our usual interpretative intervention with the poet's statement, we get a sense of what is often missing: the tonus necessary to carry the emotional reality that allows more full-bodied affective connection. Greenson (1978) points out:

> We usually pay more attention to the content of an interpretation than to its manner. The *"style,"* however, is a psychological factor of influence in its own right. It supplies both verbal and affective texture. The therapist learns the substance to interpret to his patients long before he works out the way to put it.

The basic question is: How can we get beyond the all-too-frequent reductionism of an interpretation to an apprehension of its *essence,* which we can then extend back to the patient? Much in this book addresses itself to issues of style in treatment.

Interpersonal life often assumes a complacent surface beneath which fear crouches . . . or rage stalks. The mirror of fiction offers a reflection, like an amusement park glass magnifying yet catching aspects of underlying realities. Claire Tomalin's (1988) novel *Katherine Mansfield: A Secret Life* depicts a good wife who imagines giving her husband little packets with her feelings in them, and visualizes his surprise as he opens the last packet to find it full of hatred. Couples are like cannibals. A pythonlike man invites a rabbitlike friend to share his flat, and the latter agrees meekly. Kindly old men turn into ogres, friendly women into rats, a man wanting a kiss shows a dog's teeth. Is Shirley Jackson's "Lottery," some years ago in *The New Yorker,* so unforgettable because people are unmasked as chillingly cruel behind their network of convention?

Among the countless artists who confirm Freud's findings in the unconscious, we most recently find no less a gifted perceiver than Joyce Carol Oates. In her life-long work, and now in *American Appetites* (1989), she writes about the dark underside of life that overwhelms ordinary people as well as neurotic individuals. Creative writers and clinicians join in unearthing and in knowing depiction of the powerful, irrational forces that throb below placid appearance. Among the psychotherapeutic modalities, the uncovering therapies alone are designed to descend to these depths, and there contend with these threatening feelings. It is the entire spectrum from psychoanalysis to the varied psychodynamic therapies — from Gestaltian to the Humanistic, Rankian to Eriksonian, Jungian to Sullivanian, Kohutian to Adlerian, Self Psychological to Maslowian — that this work addresses.

Hence the terms *therapist* and *analyst* are used interchangeably in this book to refer to the clinician who engages in treatment along this spectrum. I will explore the common denominator in issues of improving technique in the psychodynamic modalities, so there are few places where I need draw fine distinctions between *therapist* and *analyst.* Both terms are used to denote someone working from a psychoanalytic perspective — a perspective defined by using the transference, working through resistance and defenses, an awareness of countertransference and of the unconscious mighty waves from below that move us.

Acknowledgment

Warm appreciation is extended to Lila, wife and colleague; to Cary, son and delightful companion; and to Dr. Irving H. Paul, colleague and friend—for their keen perceptions, breadth of view, imagination, and generosity of time.

1

The Call for Connection
and Style

Failure to understand others and to be understood by them is endemic to the human condition. Such gulfs separate one person from another. Feelings are not shared much, nor for very long. Intimacy is avoided. In family life, members often attempt to "do their own thing," reaching for the security of distance, the safety of remoteness. Interpersonal relationships too often sink to levels of maintenance doses, with people living from one day to the next, one lover to the next.

In Freud's Vienna, it was *hysteria;* in the modern world *alienation* is the most prevalent problematic state experienced. Isolates adopt roles that do not truly represent them, and they accept others in *their* roles as masks to be nodded to, escaping deeper contact. Lionel Trilling, in his sensitive essay on Jane Austen's *Emma*, wrote: "There is no reality about which the modern person is more uncertain and more anxious than the reality of himself. For each of us, as for Emma, it is a sad, characteristic hope to become better acquainted with oneself." Fritz Perls, in *Eyewitness to Therapy*, extends this: "Modern man lives in a state of low-grade vitality. Though generally he does not suffer deeply, he also knows little of true creative living" (p. 12). Jean-Jacques Rousseau, in his old age and when perhaps more than a little mad, consoled himself with a daydream of a world like our own, except for the fact that its people experienced a greater closeness, and their words embraced each other's truth more. Language speaks with fuller vitality, so that feeling and knowing become one. Could we but speak in such a manner, Rousseau sighs, it would put us more closely in touch with ourselves and with one another.

In a parallel statement, John Updike (1977) asks for "something live that surfaces out of language." Those therapists who dream might also wish for just this use of language.

Our poets most closely approximate Rousseau's hopes. Joseph Brodsky (1988), in *How to Read a Book*, digresses to address his deeper interest, how to *write* a book. He cites

[poetry] as the most concise, the most condensed way of conveying the human experience. . . . [Poetry] also offers the highest possible standards for any linguistic operation.

The more one reads poetry, the less tolerant one becomes of any sort of verbosity. . . . Good style in prose is always hostage to the precision, speed and laconic intensity of poetic diction. . . . A child of epitaph and epigram, conceived indeed as a short cut, poetry to prose is a great disciplinarian.

Harry Stack Sullivan (1947) vigorously chides us, "We speak a language so esoteric that we cannot communicate with anyone outside of the profession, and we only have the illusion of communicating with each other" (p. 182).

Might not, then, Brodsky's instruction be taken to heart as profitably by the therapist as by the novelist? He adds:

I compare the difference between poetry and prose to that between the air force and the infantry. . . . Spare [yourself] a lot of useless [effort]. Poetry, one might say, has been invented for just this purpose — for it is synonymous with economy. [p. 73]

Herbert Marcuse (1989), in *One-Dimensional Man*, writes, "Art gives us a vivid, concrete experience of our condition." So does therapy. W. H. Auden (1977) has said of poetry that "we hope that someone reading it will say, 'Of course, I knew that all the time but never realized it before.' " Isn't this just what the *aha!* moment in therapy is? Interpretation is the translation by the therapist into what Frieda Fromm-Reichmann aptly termed "the language of awareness."

In the poet Robert Bly's words, "The purpose of poetry is to awaken the half of us that has been asleep for many years—to express thoughts not yet thought." That is also the purpose of therapy.

The poet, wrote Sir Philip Sidney over 300 years ago, "yeeldeth to the powers of the minde and image of that whereof the philosopher bestoweth but a wordish description." Similarly, interpretation in the clinical setting falters when the therapist becomes "wordish." Intellect, as Saul Bellow reminds us, is an excellent thing in fiction, but, like grease in a pan, it tends to congeal when the heat is turned off (Prescott 1970). In therapy, also, we strive for that intervention that connects not only with the patient's intelligence but also with his feelings and, at times, his imagination. Ezra Pound's phrase "[Man] reading should be man intensely alive" might apply equally to man in therapy, at least to man achieving successful therapeutic results.

From the creative writer, therapists can learn a communicative style—a finely chiseled clarity as in good fiction writing, and impact as in good poetry.

"The artist is a thinker whose approach is intuitive. At the top of his form, he reveals in a flash, that carries a special kind of beauty, that which others expound and analyze at length" (Wolf 1973). Might the psychotherapist approximate this? The therapist, at best, similarly plays from his own emotions, just as does the artist, employing his feelings as a radar instrument in therapy— a resonating chamber for sensing the patient, what he is and what he is about. The therapist, using the self as a sensitive instrument to reverberate to the person the patient is, positions himself, in Sullivan's words, as a *participant observer.* If we extend this concept to an *artistic participant observer,* the therapist becomes open to receive the metaphoric images of the patient as they shape themselves in the therapist's imaginative zones.[3] Sharing these images with the patient adds vitality and a sense of mutual engagement, a connection from the undercurrents of the patient tuned into by the affective strata of the therapist.[4] The patient gains a sense of actuality in the treatment process, a feeling that the therapist is more than a technician, a feeling that the therapist is responsive, empathic, and more fully there with him. And so the therapeutic process is launched.

---

[3]From the creative novelist to the creative scientist, one pivotal awareness expressed in this book has roots in what was earlier known. D. H. Lawrence observed, "Man thought and still thinks in images." Albert Einstein similarly recognized that the pictorial is basic and certainly closer to the creative zones in man. In his *Autobiographical Notes* (1946), he wrote that he arrived at his understanding by a phenomenal intuition of what the results *should* be. He tried at various times to describe what appeared to him to be distinctive about his thought processes, and in these descriptions the visual imagery, as opposed to words, is what stands out.

Conventionally expressed interpretations, we find at times, although they may be true, are often not nearly enough. When the patient's response is flat there may be many reasons, but one wonders if what might help, at times, is imagery or the leverage or the sprightliness of language.

[4]When the therapist, tuning in to the patient, feels an unmistakable tug at the fabric of his creative zones, he may reach down into his reverberations, experience there the imagery reflecting the patient's state, and share this with the patient. Applying one's imagination in order to receive a metaphor enables one to see as someone else has seen, or felt. Analyst and patient, then, send and receive on this more subtle wavelength. It is as if some kind of music goes back and forth between them (see Chapter 4).

2

Learning of Style

1. "The most tormented tragedy has been, is, and will be—the tragedy of the bedroom."

Whose insight is this? Sigmund Freud's, or a disciple's? Was it said in the earlier stage of psychoanalysis or as analysis was maturing?

Who was responsible for each of the following lines?

2. "Happy families are alike, but every unhappy family is unhappy in its own way." Was it Nathan Ackerman?
3. "Man will only become better when you make him

see what he is like." Was it Harry Stack Sullivan or
Carl Rogers?

4. "We are appalled by our own sins when we discover
   them in others."
5. "Don't be humble; you are not that great."
6. "Even in good men there is a lawless, wild-beast
   nature, which peers out in sleep."
7. "Every extension of knowledge arises from making
   conscious the unconscious."
8. "There is just so much truth the human soul can
   endure."

By now the reader has surely seen through my ploy. So I
can now add: "Those who cannot remember the past are
condemned to repeat it."

1. Actually, it was not Freud nor a Freudian who
   offered the quote concerning the tragedy of the
   bedroom, but Tolstoy. Would Freud have agreed?
   Yes, and no. Freud in 1890, yes. Freud in 1937, no.
2. Tolstoy, not a family therapist, also made the second
   observation.
3. It was Chekhov, in his *Notebooks, 1892–1904,* who
   described the confrontational technique concerning
   improving an individual by "making him see what he
   is like."
4. Goethe's "We are appalled by our own sins when we
   discover them in others" interweaves a novelist's
   anticipation of the later clinically discovered mechanisms of projective sensitivity and of reaction formation.
5. The advice "Don't be humble; you are not that great"

is not from an analyst, psychiatrist, or psychologist, but from a stateswoman, Golda Meir.

6. The awareness of the "lawless wild-beast" peering out in our sleep emanates from the fourth century B.C. Plato, in his *Republic,* anticipated a central psychoanalytic wisdom pronounced 2,200 years later. Again it was a nonclinician providing vast insights into humans — in this instance, mainly (1) an awareness of the unconscious, of its primitive, dynamic nature, expressed as the "wild-beast" within,[1] and (2) some preliminary sensing of the function of dreams that Freud was later to decipher more fully.

7. The quote that seems so psychoanalytic, "Every extension of knowledge arises from making conscious the unconscious," is actually Nietzsche's. He also noted the self can face just so much truth. Here are Sigmund Freud's themes before Sigmund Freud. If Henry James was the novelist who wrote like a psychologist, Nietzsche was surely the philosopher who did.

8. "Those who cannot remember the past are condemned to repeat it" is, of course, Santayana's.

Perceptive writers, poets, playwrights, and philosophers are often the equal, sometimes the superior, of even the most insightful therapists at uncovering the truths of human nature. At the same time, they are comparatively

---

[1]Plato wrote, "As you very well know, in [dreams] that part of the soul dares everything, as if it were loose from every shame or every sensibility. It does not hesitate to rape its mother with the imagination, or to give itself to anyone, be it man, God, or animal; no murder draws it back, no nourishment does it abstain from; there is no insensible or shameless deed it is not ready to carry out."

free of the dangers we clinicians experience of reading into our observations and are freer of any spillover from theoretical bias. Nabokov alerts us, "Inspect whether the symbol you have detected is not your own footprint" (Jong 1988). As a psychoanalyst, I am always interested in confirmations, in the *converging lines of observation* between the therapist, novelist, playwright, philosopher, and patient.

An illustration of both the secondary gains and the underlying aggression in depression comes from a playwright, Nestroy, who has one of his characters reveal, "I would not enjoy my misery half so much if I could not torture others with it." Similarly, the concepts of resistance and of defense are vivified for us by George Eliot when a created character agonizes, "One lives in peril of what may come up in the mind."

One of my favorite lines from Bernard Malamud (1971) occurs when a son advises his father to go into psychoanalysis. When the father asks why, the son answers, "To free yourself from your fate." As Eugene O'Neill explains it: "There is no present and no future — only the past, repeating itself again, and again, and again." Joseph Conrad had the same insight, but put it more wryly: "We are all loyal to the nightmare of our choice."

Freud called all this the repetition compulsion. This awareness surfaces again in modern literature. Mary McCarthy in her novel *Hannah's Needs* (1988) expresses it as: "Why do I remain loyal to the pain of childhood?" Echoing Joseph Conrad, Hannah asks, in one of the many questions that punctuate the novel, "If your heart is broken early enough, do you begin to mistake pain for love?" At the same time, the writer illuminates here something important at the center of the dynamics of masochism, that conundrum of human nature.

That writers are repeatedly discovering the truth of the repetition compulsion is also testified to by Isaac Bashevis Singer. In *The Death of Methuselah and Other Stories* (1988) the narrator says, "This is what human beings are. This is their history, and I am afraid this is also their future."

On the bookshelf, in fruitful juxtaposition, Freud's *Civilization and Its Discontents* and Nietzsche's *Thus Spake Zarathustra* may stand as penetrating psychological statements. The former—even though from Freud himself—is arguably no more so than the other. The philosopher offers us a breathtakingly monumental contribution to understanding depth psychology, second only to that of the discoverer of psychoanalysis on his home ground.

Few clinicians can pick up as sensitively as the creative writers the meaning that networks an individual's emotions or fragments of behavior, or the underlying pattern and plight of a life. It is literature that brings the human experience, with all of its complex diversity, into sharpest possible focus.[2]

If psychology, psychiatry, and psychoanalysis were to solve their differences and join together in one ideological house, and were to engrave over its entranceway the signature phrase by which all who enter might draw inspiration, which truth offered by them could supersede one contributed by another discipline? The Socratic

---

[2]There are areas of understanding of deeper psychology for which Freud, for one, recognized the writer as providing the greater illumination. He conceded that his own views on femininity were "incomplete and fragmentary" and advised us then to "turn to the poet" to learn more.

adage, "The unexamined life is not worth living" certainly
edges out other contending statements; unless we give the
nod to another Greek maxim, "Find out who you are;
then be that person."

Perhaps only Freud, from among the analysts, can
stand with Shakespeare, Tolstoy, Dostoevsky, Schopen-
hauer, Nietzsche, Goethe, Proust, Chekhov, and others
the reader might nominate, in the profundity of the
illuminations offered — or can stand even with those on a
lower rung defined by Honoré Balzac, Victor Hugo,
François-Marie Voltaire, James Joyce, Franz Kafka,
Henry James, Thomas Mann, T. S. Eliot, Somerset
Maugham, Mark Twain, Tennessee Williams, and Ar-
thur Miller. As we well know, even Freud's towering
contribution of the Oedipus triangle was keenly anticipated by Sophocles, as was another of his sweeping
conceptions earlier pronounced in Wordsworth's "the
child is father of the man."

Language

The analyst uses words. Words are his one and only tool
in the "talking cure." But generally we don't tend to use
our tool in a refined way, with precision, effectiveness,
and, at indicated times, evocativeness. The creative
writer does. From him we may learn to return substance
to a language too often pureed by its everyday use; from
him we may learn to use words to lift feelings into
awareness.

In our work, the words are seldom right; too often
they strip language of life or offer communication that
bypasses the patient to come to rest in a junkyard of stale
metaphors. The therapist, coming as he does from an

academic background, is trained to turn living feelings into concepts. This juiceless process is nowhere more destructive than when working with an obsessive-compulsive patient, whose central defense is to shut out the pulsing currents of affect, whose therapy process reduces itself to a steady slogging through airless session after session after session.

How does one escape from this maze, still enlivened, enlivening, and lucid? Artists may help us. Refreshing the dialogue with the patient may replace our mental loitering, our mutual lassitude when it threatens to settle in at some phases of the work, particularly in the long middle stretch of treatment, when feelings may slide toward the repetitious, when the ground is all too familiar and the involvement hollows and loses its zing. Along with the central process of understanding and interpreting the transference and countertransference dynamics that feed this sluggishness, might we not use language more artfully to freshen the patient's involvement in the process of connecting both with himself and with the therapist?

Depressive patients join the obsessive-compulsive ones in profiting from a vitalizing tone in the therapeutic atmosphere. An enlivening style is therapeutic for the analyst as well as for the patient, in that the depressive's despondency and despair, or the obsessive's rarefied emotional atmosphere, work *on* the therapist no less than they neurotically work *for* the patient.

In his *Writings on the Theatre* (1964), Eugene Ionesco shares with us, "For me art means the revelation of certain things that reason, everyday habits of thought, conceal from me," and then adds, "Art pierces everyday reality. It springs from a different state of mind." Ionesco's insight suggests that like the analyst's interpretation, art aims to get into the psychological beneath the logical. At the same time, the observation joins current scientific research concerning the right-brain and left-brain functions. This convergence of observations from art and science has both confirming reassurance and clinical implications. The left hemisphere deals with facts, logic, deduction, learning; the right brain with feeling, fantasy, imagination, imagery, and intuition, and is the site of the artistic and creative. Classroom teaching calls predominantly upon the left hemisphere, and play calls upon the right.

While therapy seeks to integrate the operation of left- and right-brain hemispheres, much of the deeper work involves engaging the right hemisphere. It is the right brain for the most part that must be unfettered to free the patient from his constraints. Thus, to talk the language of the right brain is to put one closer to the zone that is to receive the message if anything is to happen.

Hence, prose logic and poetic thought tend to be received by the different hemispheres. "The difference between prose logic and poetic thought," says Robert Graves in *Genius* (1984), "is that the logician uses words as a builder uses bricks, involving a comparative unemotional deadness, whereas the poet deals with words as living creatures."

Empathic participation and the awareness of the interfering effects of wordiness are acquisitions of a psychotherapist's seasoning. Appelbaum (1977), in his chapter "A Psychoanalyst Looks at Gestalt Therapy," makes a similar observation when he speaks of "the discrimination between ideas and ideation, between well-worn obsessional pathways and new thoughts, between a

statement of experience and a statement of a statement."
If there is one thing the psychodynamic schools of
therapy hold in common regarding the theory of technique, it is that insights are effective only when they are
accompanied by, or wedded to, affect. Even the last
bastion of the emphasis on the rational in interpretation,
Albert Ellis's theory, has moved toward the affect and
signals this in its name change from *Rational Therapy* to
Rational-Emotive Therapy. Ellis, too, lately joins the view
that illumination offered the patient, even if it is valid, is
not nearly enough. Conventionally expressed interpretations often emphasize abstract meaning, and such interpretations replace the experience with its deciphering,
another way of robbing that experience of its emotional
authenticity. "The patient is in need of an experience,"
Frieda Fromm-Reichmann (1950) puts it, "not an explanation."

I recall a young college student patient who was
being tossed and turned by a heavy transference neurosis.
"Analysis," he said, half-indicting himself for finding it
hard to take and half-indicting the treatment process,
"really hurts. Why has it become so difficult?" Between
the lines I heard another question: "Do you know my
distress?" What was needed, therefore, was more than an
explanation — some demonstration. The explanation
might suffice for his manifest question. The latent plea
needed something more.

"Reliving your childhood here," I commented, resonating to what he was going through, "opens old wounds,
spilling fresh blood." Then he knew I had a sense of his
pain, not from a text on transference, but from something more personal. And it vividly — affectfully — clarified his experience for him, focusing his feelings and

giving that experience meaning that made it somewhat more endurable.

Therapy should move toward the earthy — the meat and potatoes of real feelings — toward the affectively actual. (Although, with some patients, the schizoid for example, this progression must proceed with exquisite slowness.) A sense of what I mean by earthy may be found not only in the previous example but in the arts as well. The following discourse on the use of words in creative writing may be examined for its relevance to our use of words in therapy: "There is language that plunges in, not too proud to steal a noise from Mother Nature," says novelist Paul West (1988). He then explains, and adds a note on the origin and potential power of words:

> This plunge is almost like revisiting our ancestors. After all, words must have begun as acts of abstract approximation, a simultaneous closeness and removedness that nabbed the essence of a thing in a shout, a grunt, a hiss, but partly in order to refer to it in general. . . . [The appropriate words] will perhaps restore the shielded, abstracted modern reader to that more atavistic state of mind. It is not a matter of coming up with new words, but fiercer — of coming up with new and more imposing combinations of words. [page 10]

West, here, might equally address this instruction to the therapist as to the writer, since both pursue the goal of connecting with feelings. It is here that we may restore the echo, at least, of the shout, or grunt, or hiss to the patient's experience.

Aldous Huxley (1963) concurs with such a need and shows us that one task challenging the therapist is strikingly like one facing the artist:

> Regarding the task confronting every serious writer, it is only by an unusual combination of purified words that our

private experiences in all their subtlety, in their unrepeated uniqueness can be, in some sort, *re-created* and made communicable. [italics added]

In my work I may often aim for something analogous: to re-create in this way, by picking out the essence of the patient's communicated experience and presenting it back, as does the novelist who moves us, so that the patient can fully feel his own submerged issues in living when they are extracted and held up to him. But if the patient only sees it, that is not enough. He must, as he would in reading good writing, resonate to it. Then he knows it as his own, or else it will be just a story he is told.

For our therapy purposes we can learn especially from the masters of rich prose, from Joyce, Faulkner, Dillon, Wallace Stevens, and Nabokov to reach for the full-bodied word, and not to be afraid to stretch at times, if it will better serve, for the plump image, succulent, and touched with novelty. Or we might learn from writers like Hemingway how to be sparse, direct, clean.

The significant writers, as well as the more able therapists, are available as mentors from whom to draw for our technique. To bypass the former is to overlook one of two potential sources of rare tutelage.

The trick is fitting the style to the type of patient (see Chapter 8, "Style for Specific Disorders"), although another consideration is which style is more congenial to which therapist and which he can more naturally incorporate into his own.

The Texture of an Interpretation

Interpretation should be addressed toward that potential self-awareness that hovers, sometimes lurks, just out of sight. In terms of timing, it might be offered at that particular moment when what is going on beneath presses up toward, yet can't quite break into, the experiential surface. In terms of place, the interpretation is most usable when offered in response to the patients' patterns in living when these patterns get activated *in* the therapy session.

As to how? The intervention ideally carries fiber as well as shape. The poets instruct that such fiber calls into play the patient's senses. An imaged communication has this advantage. Sometimes it effectively clarifies, but beyond this it may send something home in a way that really registers with the patient. One woman in treatment engaged in rapid chatter without pause. This prevented me from expressing any observations, and it did not allow any unbidden thoughts to emerge from her and take her by surprise. I interrupted one day to say that her defense seemed much like that of a "sentry rapidly doing double-time to allow no one across the border from either side." The idea had earlier been expressed to her without this image, but with its assistance, she was able to sense more clearly what she was doing. Her speech settled to a more natural pace and treatment could proceed. She had been able, as are other patients, to try on the image more easily than she could mere words. If the image then fits, a deeper connection with, and taking in, the interpreted meaning results.

One middle-aged patient gave full meaning to the concept of *masochism*. Minor troubles were elevated to moderate ones, and moderate ones to tragedy. She resisted acknowledging anything positive and would string together complaint after complaint. Once, as I walked her to the door after a session, and aware of a delightfully balmy first spring day after a rather miserable winter, I commented, "Do enjoy this lovely day." Quick as, actually *quicker* than, a wink, she shot back, "What, and step in all the dog shit in New York?" Inasmuch as this exchange occurred on her way out, there was no opportunity to deal with its meaning then. But later in the treatment I formulated for her the picture she conveyed: "Much like a promising stone that comes to a master sculptor, troubles falling into your hands are assured of being rendered into their fullest." This gave her pause, intrigued her, and evoked a more considered, extended consideration of her masochistic pattern than she had as yet ever undertaken.

One male patient had ideas that tended to remain consistently tentative, unfocused, and dim. Once after about a year of therapy, he feebly, cautiously dared to express an opinion. For the first time in our relationship he ventured out of his characterological role of appeasing compliance. He had always been afraid that he would either anger someone or else appear foolish. I shared with him a broad observation: "A man afraid of ever saying a foolish thing never says a brilliant one." This principle for more courageous living, offered in the context of a rich transference in which his assertion was not punished but approved, invited further efforts at self expression as he took it forward into his relationships, in therapy and out. He appeared now to use his current father figure's Polonius-like advice to his son to replace his actual father's earlier admonition: "Children should be seen and not heard."

The clear note I sounded combined content and style to give endorsement to the more imaginative and colorful that he had not yet allowed himself in life. He learned thereby to open up his own expressiveness and gradually to extend himself more vividly. He progressed to where he could put things as incisively as he later said, "I felt obliged for everything I was ever given. It was like my parents put up a neon sign in my room, flashing 'YOU'LL PAY FOR THIS.'"

Semrad (Rako and Mazer 1988) works in the same way. His responses to patients are aphoristically simple and elegant. For example: "The only fuel for learning is the sadness you feel from your mistakes. It's important not to waste this fuel." Or, "It's a necessary condition of health to be able to bear what has to be borne, to be able to think what has to be thought."

Once in group therapy, I realized that one of our members would invariably move, in one relationship after another, into an argumentative, combative mode, with the consequent disruption leading to the relationship's termination. She was beginning to have similar fights with group members—this one was "criticizing" her, that one "misunderstanding" her, another "mistreating" her, still another giving her unwanted "advice," and so on. After a while, it became clear that this was a smoke-screen. Behind this screen, she was actually using the fights as a means of connection, as a variety of intimacy. With her pathologically jealous mother, it had been a hidden means of connection with her father and brothers. It repeated itself in the group; she was covertly enjoying the attention and the relating, while manifestly now it was the whole group that "did not understand" or was "criticizing" her, and things began moving into the negative cycle that she had made her own. An analogy came to my mind, with which I then reached through to her. It was of her "being given food she liked, but spitting

out some of each mouthful in mocked disgust in order to
secretly swallow for herself some portion of each bite."
That made it meaningful—and feelingful, giving life to a
dry concept. And this combination of clarification and
affective quality, her reaction demonstrated, made it
digestible.[3]

Therapeutic Goal

What is it that constitutes the structural changes in the
patient undergoing psychodynamic treatment? The conventional view is that the improving, and improved,
patient changes by finding modulated avenues of handling impulses more constructively, and developing an
altered relationship among four entities: the mastery-
seeking ego that had earlier balanced too precariously in
its role among the turbulent id, the admonitory superego,
and insistent reality. To contribute to all this, insight
must be taken beyond understanding to a fuller *emotional
acceptance* of the impulses. This self acceptance joins the
processes leading to a stronger ego and a more tolerant
superego—both drawing upon some positive identification with the analyst and an incorporation of his way of
looking at the patient, a manner of viewing in which
acceptance replaces self condemnation and in which guilt
gives way to self tolerance.

To help patients gain this acceptance of their conflictual impulses, the analyst's maintenance of a nonjudg-
mental posture is essential, particularly when this stance

---

[3]For other clinical examples of the theme of this chapter, the reader is
referred to Chapters 5, 6, and 7 where it is approached from a different
perspective.

extends to the illumination of the transference. Strachey (1934) focused on the concept that there is little that can ease superego tyranny as much as the patient's experiencing, in the living treatment, that he can express ideas and, even more important, feelings that he regards as unacceptable. This is most effective when directed toward the analyst without the latter (now wearing the parental transference) responding with criticality, punitiveness, or judgmentalness. As we will see in later chapters, I propose that growth is all the more extended if the patient can experience his once superego-condemned impulses, sometimes *in front* of the analyst, more importantly *toward* the analyst, and experience *from* the analyst not only the conventional acceptance, but a joyful receiving of the humanness of such impulses. Can the patient now be led not only to a capacity for love and work, but toward an even higher attainment, an exuberance in love and work?

Capping a distinguished career combining psychotherapy research and practice, Hans Strupp (1989) sorts out the functional gains from therapy. What can be expected are: (1) improvements in interpersonal functioning; (2) increases in self-esteem, self-confidence, security, self-respect, and personal worth; (3) greater interest in living, energy, and satisfaction; (4) a greater sense of mastery and competence; and (5) significant diminution of the problems (symptoms) that brought the patient to therapy.

The third factor comes close to what we should ideally extend to our patients, but it doesn't go far enough. Beyond—well beyond—"greater interest in living, energy, and satisfaction" exists a potential for a still healthier thrust, one closer to the very richness of existence itself. The analyst can assist the patient in going beyond a mere *tolerance* of his deeper self toward a rejoicing in and an actual *celebration* of the deeper dimensions, a giving way to the fluidity and evanescence of life, much as do certain poets. Then the patient might not only ease pain and escape from distress, but more affirmatively, find a capacity for verve, for buoyancy, and for earthiness. Thoreau refers to this as "to be alive, to the extremities." Joyce Carol Oates calls it "to live one's life passionately." Edith Wharton terms it a "life-lover, life-wonderer and emotional adventurer." Shelley puts it more expansively: "boundless, as we wish our souls to be." H. L. Mencken expresses it as attaining the state where "the good red sun does not send one scurrying." And Milan Kundera, lyrically, albeit ambivantly, calls it the "unbearable lightness of being."

The Therapist

The professional comes to psychoanalytic training, generally, from medicine, psychology, and social work. But, in our conventional thinking, do we overlook another fruitful source, the person trained in literature and the classics, in the thoughtful study of character in depth, of relationships and their subtleties,[4] and, at the same time,

---

[4]Like the psychodynamic therapist, the creative writer is fascinated by what personality tries to hide from us in its deep pleats and pockets and is good at loosening its folds enough to glimpse what may be inside. The novelist's ability to capture people's inner, in addition to their outer, voices sympathetically is often unerring and precise. How often in the clinical literature do we find the subtlety of interpersonal processes so exquisitely detailed, accompanied by so sensitive a pairing out of undercurrents, as in the following brief example (Currie 1986)?

of the nuances of language? Should such a candidate be a writer, all the better! The selective process of these latter candidates for psychoanalytic training bring the probability of fuller endowments of intuition, and of sensibility for resonating to human situations. Such candidates might also be more ready to develop and to draw upon the artistic — even the creative — within them for their therapeutic endeavor.[5]

Chessick (1983) speaks of therapists who ignore the use of anything of artistic potential within themselves for their work. He refers to the psychiatrist who, in darting away from the intuitive, wears a white coat and identifies firmly with the medical establishment. Hollingshead and

---

A woman complained that her father is driving her mad by telling her to "keep in touch." He is a patient in a nursing home, a rancorous man on the outs with almost everyone almost all of the time. She's a good and tender woman and a dutiful daughter. He has always been a distant, cranky father. She visits and telephones him frequently but never escapes, she says, without his telling her to "keep in touch." Sometimes it sounds like an accusation; sometimes a plea; sometimes a taunt. Maybe it's what he uses for "I love you."

The novelist's sure sense of people suggests that both student and established therapist might be well advised to not spend all of one's available time for reading on clinical material alone, but to divide the precious allotment between the psychodynamic fare and serious literature. The artistic works may be studied (and enjoyed) as Freud did, for understanding of personality. He learned, as we will now learn, the value of artistic imagery. His work in therapy and his writing both were enlivened with metaphors and also with reference to novels and to plays, and on occasion to poetry.

[5]I was pleased recently to find a kindred spirit in a psychiatrist-psychoanalyst, Robert Seidenberg (1989): "If it ever came to a point that psychoanalysis had to be entrusted to anyone, my vote would go to a professor of English. By training and experience, such a person knows about metaphors and their meaning in the human experience . . . [about] words and abstractions, . . . [and] the symbolic process."

Redlich (1958) refer to this group as "directive and organic therapists." Such clinicians lean toward giving drugs, electric shock, somatic therapy, and advice. A similar type of psychologist joins this side, following rigid experimental schools and attempting to force psychotherapy along certain theoretical lines, hoping to keep the personal aspects of the therapeutic relationship to a minimum.

Another type of therapist adheres dogmatically, cultishly, to the theories produced by one of the giants, whether Freud, Jung, Adler, Klein, Sullivan, Horney, Reich, Erikson, or Kohut.

To these categories we might add others. Psychotherapy may be viewed as a ladder that runs from the ground to the sky, from the scientific to the artistic. The best therapist takes a midway position, but this position is as much a function of temperament as of theoretical belief. The middle position encompasses a capacity for both tough-minded and tender-minded approaches, for oscillating between obsessive-compulsive and hysteroid potentials in oneself, without getting stuck at either polarity.

Overemphasis on the scientific and tough-minded obsessional qualities in the therapist incurs the risk that the therapeutic experience will be reduced to an intellectual, detached exercise. Actual behavioral change for the patient never gets off the ground. At best, the process remains somewhat academic; at worst, weighed down by tedium and pedantry.

On the other hand, too much artistry that is tender-minded in quality and hysteroid in emotional tone results in treatment that is impressionistic and impulsive. It results in the therapist's opening a cauldron of insuffi-

ciently understood variables onto the therapeutic situation. Intuition—if not appropriately balanced by the
critical faculties shaping, selecting, and evaluating responses before they are released—produces a disruptive,
disturbing experience for the patient. The patient may
not stand still in therapy, but neither should he be
chaotically tossed in many directions at once. There is no
patterning of processes initiated and refined; there is little
unfolding of a direction. It may become a bit like a
painting done by a chimpanzee—all random impulse,
undirected by a guiding intelligence. (In Rorschach
terminology, the process is that of *color* and *color-form*
without the balancing effect of sufficient *form-color*. One
thinks of that brand of existentialist who shares even his
"pathology" with the patient. Conversely, domination of
the therapist by the "scientist" part of himself results in a
treatment situation that leans toward being all form
without any enlivening of the process by a form-color
response.)

To approximate creative and full personhood within
the therapist's role (and can anyone considerably less than
a full person assist patients to become full individuals?),
it is essential to know how and when to temporarily
suspend one's logic. It is a precondition to suspend
momentarily an ever-evaluative, criticizing, judging function of the mind. This is necessary in order to remain
open to "receiving" uncritically the off-beat experience or
the unexpected surprising idea. Then, of course, the
therapist must bring his critical functions back into play
to evaluate the new perceptions—to select those that make
sense and those he judges appropriate and helpful to
share with the patient. The more gifted therapist is the
one who is capable of loosening the brakes that hold back
the irrational. Only then does he reactivate the critical

functions to shape, to modify, or to discard. He must be capable of recalling this critical side, or the process degenerates into "wild" psychotherapy.

To remain too "scientific," to maintain an unyielding heavy rationality may inhibit the appearance of the unerring intuitive hunch. Only when these hunches play their appropriate part in the process does psychoanalysis become more than the mere exercise of a craft; only then does it attain the level of a creative endeavor.[6]

To be creative, one has to be able to peel off and *momentarily* lay aside one's sensible layers. Otherwise, one stays, as a therapist, and as a person, one of those "reasonable" people who, as mentioned previously, never offer a silly idea, nor a brilliant one.

On the other hand, let us not overlook the possibilities of either extreme, the all-scientist or the all-artist type who may happen to be right for a *particular* type of patient. For the highly confused, labile patient who could profit from a process assisting him in "binding" himself, the scientist type of therapist may prove helpful. For the detached, encapsulated, schizoid, or obsessional patient, the all-artist therapist might be right for liberating affect, for thawing out feeling, and for attaching the patient to a

---

[6]This point invites a few remarks beyond the special circumstances of the therapy room. Unrelieved rationality inhibits originality and imagination. Continuous rationality stifles the appearance of a novel, incredible, or "unheard of" perception; yet, this is what creativity really is—the *reception* of a new, fresh idea that is so preposterous that no one ever conceived of such a likelihood before. After all, it was just a "mad" idea that the world is not flat but round; that we are descended from a common ancestor to the monkey; that the earth is not the center of the universe with the sun revolving around it; that there is an unconscious part of us; that our blood circulates rather than stays still; that it is intercourse which leads to a baby nine months later. Imagine how the caveman who came up with *that* one was hooted out of the communal cave!

meaningful life experience—if such a therapist proceeds
with self-awareness and some balancing of his personality
bent.

The scientist–artist blend in a therapist is what is
most effective for most patients, and offers the greatest
versatility of approach and of resources in treatment
strategy. No less importantly, it goes along with the
therapist's possessing authentic *range* as a person in the
therapeutic exchange.[7]

Should therapy provide the patient with windows to
look through or environs to react in? The most effective
therapist is the one capable of supplying either—when,
and to whom, appropriate. The therapist must be flexible
enough to shift between the polarities of Sullivan's
participant-observer role. The therapist should know
when and how to move toward the "blank screen" posture
in treatment, but he should also be capable of what I
might term *educated spontaneity*—that is, the ability to
selectively express his own feelings when appropriate and
contributory to the goals of the treatment.

The art of being is an art of balance. Antithetical
impulses must be held in dynamic equilibrium. At neither
polarity does one encounter the complexity, the creative
tension, nor the capacity for vision we hope for in those
who would be psychotherapists. What is needed is a
balanced mixture of the art and the science of psychotherapy and a mixture of art and science in the psychotherapist.

---

[7]It is this capacity for active use of intellect *and* affect, and for experiencing
a harmonious balance between the two, that, as a faculty member of
psychoanalytic training institutes, I look for in candidates. It is this use of
both scientific and artistic sides, perhaps as much as any other goal, which
we might strive to help analysts-in-training to liberate.

3

Fundamentals
of Style

In the quest for the most effective way to express an underlying understanding, how can the therapist best present to the patient the difficult truths of his nature? How can the therapist best put him in touch with the complexities of his defenses and with that against which he defends himself? How can the therapist best move him, step by step, to the authenticity of his feelings, to the real, and the more real?

What ingredients should an ideal interpretation possess? An interpretation should carry no surplus words, no excess baggage, and should have a precision of form and logic. It should be expressed at a time the patient can hear it and in a manner to which the patient can resonate. Thus, the therapist would speak to the immediate and the personal, responding with what he sees and feels just beyond the patient's awareness.

The interpretation should have the benefit of vividness. It should be a refined statement, eliciting feelings that connect fully and freshly with the patient. It should possess a sense of truth to the patient's state, and it should be one step in a process of steady movement toward the center of a genuine experience. The interpretation would be given in the midst of an actual occurrence, and would further constitute a *related* actual event of its own, so that the patient can more readily assimilate it. This assimilation would, in turn, enable an expansion of a dimension of the known self. The patient's participation in the intervention would, in the long run, make some contribution to a life enhanced by this newly discovered relationship.

All this is a pretty tall order. But the ideal is a distant star toward which to aim, an aspiration toward which to strive. My comments may suggest to some readers that, beyond the empirical findings that interpretations "work," (and certainly stronger than any experimental data), perhaps there is also a personal attraction that draws therapists to embrace an interpretative approach. To follow Samuel Butler, interpretation, like life, "is the art of drawing sufficient conclusions from insufficient premises."

It is the therapist's purpose to share his awareness in a form the patient can hear. The phrasing of interpretations is a question of style, a question of how something is put, and of the meaning of that how. We usually pay more attention to the content of an interpretation than to the manner in which it is stated. However, the style is a psychological factor of influence in its own right. It supplies both verbal and affective texture. The apprentice therapist learns the substance to interpret to his patients, but he is more on his own in learning the *way* to put it, the technique of shaping a careful, usable interpretation. Levy (1963) speaks of style as a "personal element . . . which may, in the final analysis, differentiate between the successful and the unsuccessful, the mediocre and the brilliant . . . and may often count for as much as, if not more than, content in making the difference."

Style, however, is a function not only of one's personality, but even of one's transient mood: exuberant or dampened, playful or somber, energetic or passive, whimsical or matter-of-fact, expansive or constricted. In constructing the therapeutic relationship, the therapist inevitably draws on his own way of being and his particular method of making relationships work (even if on theoretical grounds he feels he should not); in so doing, he endows the relationship with some tone of consequence. Particularly interesting in this regard is Freud's comment on the therapist's personal involvement; he writes that one should "not entirely give up one's personal note" (Meng and E. Freud 1964).

Within the scope allowed by one's personality and mood, one may call forth something that exists within, can give license to the emergence of one or another component. A therapist shapes his own style from the interaction of his personality with his experience. Are there any common denominators left when experiences are pooled and the individual elements subtracted? Are there any guidelines to be distilled, even in terms of style, that, if they cannot quite be taught, can at least be passed on as hints to those who have the particular potentials for one or another style? Probably there are. If an art can't exactly be taught, at least a direction can be pointed for those who can follow.

Style is the manner of a communication, not its matter. Yet the distinction between manner and matter is a slippery one; manner affects matter. Donald Hall, the poet, discussing this issue in a literary context (1967), points out that one linguist took Caesar's "I came — I saw — I conquered" and revised it to "I arrived on the scene of the battle; I observed the situation; I won the victory." Here the matter is the same, but Caesar's arrogant dignity disappears into the pallid pedantry of the longer version. It is impossible to say that the matter is unaffected.

Colby (1951) conveys this concentrated advice: "Effective interpretations are concise, simply phrased, and few in number, begin as approximations on the periphery, and end as convergences on the center" (p. 90).

Interpretations are most effective when they are both astringent and tender — that is, *astringent in content and tender in manner,* when the therapist's calling it as he sees it is combined with some sympathetic tuning in on the receiving patient. In speaking of desirable qualities in those who work with the mind, Plato similarly mentioned boldness and benevolence.

An interpretation is more usable and more likely to touch feelings if aimed toward a point of emotional relevance — that is, toward what the patient is experiencing right *now,* not what he experienced last session or outside the session. This is not to say that reference to what happened previously should not be combined with reference to what is happening currently. But there is little therapeutic advantage in going back to a stale past occurrence when it is not echoing in some event in the present. This is one reason that transference interpretations are more mutative than other interpretations.

The underlying model is one of collaborators working with each other, not a doctor working on a patient. "The analyst should be," as Robertiello and colleagues (1963) put it, "a human being working *with* another human being, not doing something *to* another human being" (p. 119). On the basis of this model, interpretative *possibilities* offered to the patient might convey a certain tentativeness. Therefore the therapist would do well to begin an interpretation with some phrase like "Could it be that . . ." or "Perhaps . . ." This offers three advantages: (1) It permits the patient to refute an interpretation with less timidity or fear of threatening the relationship; (2) it allows the patient to more easily revise an interpretation or accept part and reject another part; and (3) it puts the patient in an active, collaborative posture in the treatment enterprise, rather than defining him as a passive recipient of treatment.

Similarly, if the patient gives a rationalization, the therapist might say, "Yes, and for what other reasons?" Or, "Yes, and what else?" This does not make the patient feel that he is viewed as a liar, and yet does not make the therapist seem naive. At the same time, it moves the patient forward toward the more basic issues behind the secondary reason he initially offered, the real reasons behind the "good" reasons. And it initiates a process for the long run of learning to recognize the truth by how deeply one longs to disbelieve it.

Another suggestion is to employ the patient's own words wherever possible: *mishigass* for his obsession, *habit* if this is the way he refers to his tic, *fiddling* as the child may term his masturbating, and so on.

On the other hand, in those instances where the patient is euphemizing, the therapist might be instructed not to accept the patient's term, but to employ a more direct one. If the patient says, "We were doing it," the therapist might ask, "Intercourse?" or use the vernacular; and if the patient refers to someone's "passing away," the therapist might use the more direct term "died." The therapist should demonstrate that the facts of human experience are not to be avoided, that issues or feelings can be addressed without prissiness—close up, not at arm's length. Thus the therapist, in his directness, sets an example for the patient in honest self-expression. In the process, the patient might come to find that this principle of authenticity extends to many things. It applies to his no longer having to think in such terms as "I didn't *mean* to hurt your feelings" when hostility seeps through. It means not resorting to generalities in order to attribute to no one in particular opinions that one is unwilling to call one's own. It means not disguising lack of feeling by clichés that purport to display feeling.

Thus the intent is to break through the barrier of the surface noises people ordinarily make to fend off relating. In the therapeutic experience, the patient is exposed to the hard reality, on both sides, of genuine statements. He thereby eventually learns to truly communicate "of himself." He gains the courage to tell it like it is.

The therapist should be taught early to stay away not only from technical words, but from formal words as well. Aristotle, in his *Rhetoric,* advises, "Clearness is secured by using the words . . . that are current and ordinary." Rather than speaking of the patient's need to be "controlling," the therapist might refer to his need to "call the shots" or to "hold the reins," particularly if the patient is not well educated. Even with sophisticated patients, rather than saying "compulsive," the therapist might speak of the patient's "liking everything in its place before he begins" when he straightens the ashtray and then arranges himself fastidiously on the couch. The advantage is that this style is more personal and closer to the patient's feelings; it conveys a sense that the therapist is speaking *of* the patient, not from a textbook.

Beyond using the patient's own words when possible, and common parlance at all times, we must translate our observations into the patient's concrete experience, if we are to reach him more than intellectually. We might adopt the patient's characteristic phrases in the interests of furthering an intimate, personal communication system, much like that which develops between long-time friends. The common, private, "in-group" aspects of language established between patient and therapist afford not only short cuts, but also a more affect-toned idiom and a closeness in communicative exchange. It is thus helpful for the therapist to know and use the particular phrases that trigger those special images and meanings to which the patient most personally relates. *It is the patient's imagery, even more than the therapist's that is therapeutically usable.*[1]

Some patients do not at first generate imagery, but this capacity for expansiveness is often developed in the course of treatment. Until the patient develops such creative capacity, however, there is an intermediate

---

[1]This is true, in spite of all I will have to say in the following two chapters on the special value of the therapist's images in the treatment process.

alternative — that of the analyst "hearing," discerning, the patient's own unexpressed metaphors and then formulating them.

One woman in treatment had been brought up by a mother who always gave her, beneath acceptable dresses, shabby and torn undergarments to wear, relegated her to the least expensive activities, and saved money on small things for her daughter as well as large — this in spite of the fact that the family was financially quite comfortable. As an adult, the patient felt guilty whenever she took pains with her appearance, whenever she obtained a good grade in school, whenever she accomplished or succeeded at any endeavor. Relating to this, I commented: "Could it be you feel afraid when you dare to dress well, not in the *torn underwear* your mother prescribed?" She experienced a flash of connection in which she suddenly *really* knew what she had "known" all along. This was an "aha!" moment, beyond seeing — the *feeling* of an underlying reality.

A young man who had been brought up in an Orthodox Jewish family now felt guilty for having become a graduate psychology student and for having entered analysis. He said, "My parents don't want me to look inward."

"Only look upward?" I asked, referring to God and spirituality.

He immediately responded to the shorthand developed between us: "Yes, or else look to the side." His statement implied denial and selective perception, but was expressed without psychologizing. What is important in the treatment of psychologists, psychiatrists, or clinical students in treatment is to pull them away from academic and technical terms, to have them talk (and to talk to them) in the language they spoke before they entered professional training.

A patient who was a writer had once been in prison and, for a short time, in solitary. He now described an experience there with his writer's refined artistic appreciation:

> One evening, feeling terribly alone, I looked out the small window, yearning for a view of someone or of anything. I saw only a few lights from other windows. There was nothing else to be seen. My emptiness increased, and I felt it all unbearable. Gradually, gradually, I began to look somewhat differently at the corner of the yard which I could see, and I began to see differentiations, shades of darkness, shadows and light. The dark and light formed interesting designs. Things slowly changed, bit by bit. I saw more and more. The whole scene began to come through a sharper filter, more vivid, a montage of angles and lines and light. As my perception changed, my feelings followed. I felt relieved, a bit excited. I looked for a long time, luxuriating in something fresh I could see where before there was only the tired view and my numbness. My mind returned to life.

This experience was conveyed to me early in our consultation. He shortly thereafter moved from the chair to the analytic couch, and I explained how he might undertake the free-associative process. In so doing, I reached back to his own experience and asked him to now look out a similar window: to sense, and share with me, all he saw, the patterns, shades, shadows and light through the window that opened onto his childhood, his current relationships, his feelings toward me, all other feelings, his physical sensations, and so on.

Another way for the analyst to orient patients to free

association is to quote Matisse who is said to have given the instruction to new apprentices: Go and "see a flower for the first time."[2]

I currently use this window image (which I had asked the patient to write out for me for such use) with other patients as well, adding the elaboration — borrowing from Freud's metaphor of looking out a train window — to report whatever is seen to some companion to whom the scene is not available to view. This image, to my mind, has some advantage over Freud's, adding as it does an element of illustrating and inviting the mobilization of exquisitely fine attention to the subtlest textures of experience.

A male patient, who entered therapy because his impotence was interfering with his marriage, had lost his father when he was 7 years old. The man his mother married shortly thereafter wore a prosthetic device in place of a missing hand. When therapy was under way, the patient seemed to explore whatever the therapist said in order to underscore the therapist's capability, knowledge, perceptiveness, and mastery. The patient appeared to be looking consistently and *closely* for the positive aspects. At one point, when there was cause to refer to this, I phrased it in terms of the patient's desire to reassure himself that I had "two good hands." This said it for the patient, briefly and particularly meaningfully, affectfully and out of his experience.

A similar effect was obtained in the following in-

[2]From another creative modality, Ernest Hemingway echoes the same attitude: "All my life I've looked at words as though I were seeing them for the first time."

stance. A young man was quite ambivalently involved in competitive relationships with peers and in rivalry with an intimidating father. His father had been a professional minor-league baseball player and had pressured his son to play in Little League and then on the high school and college baseball teams. When the patient's acute rivalrous wishes and fears were reexperienced toward me in the transference, the comment that he seemed to be contending "to see who had the more powerful bat" was something to which he could emotionally relate. *When interpreting, we must, if we are to reach our patients, retranslate meanings back into their specific experiences.*

As an extension of this point, the basic precondition for psychotherapy is that therapist and patient speak the same language. I remember an incident years ago when, as an intern, I was asked to fill out a research form on an adolescent patient in the hospital. I asked him, when I came to that question, whether he had ever had intercourse.

"No," he said.

Something about him stirred in my mind, and I asked, "Have you ever been laid?"

"Oh yes, lots of times, since I was 14."

I've remembered this lesson. When an adolescent in group therapy jumps up to punch another, an analyst should have ready at hand the words "Cool it!" We can sense how much more authority there is in speaking the patient's language at this critical moment than there would be in the words "No fighting allowed." Speaking the patient's vernacular allows the therapist to step closer to the patient when this is suddenly (or otherwise) needed.

4

Poetic Style: Use of Imagery

Metaphor is a means for reaching the unconscious.

Gorelick (1989)

(Metaphor connects with) the other rivers that lie/lower, that touch us only in dreams/ . . . we feel their tug/As a dowser's rod bends to the source below.

Cox and Theilgard (1986)

The task of the poet is expressed by A. E. Housman (1933): "I think that to transfuse emotions — not to transmit thought but to set up in the reader's sense a vibration corresponding to what was felt by the writer — is the particular function of poetry" (p. 18). Ruesch (1961), in *Therapeutic Communication,* writes:

> It is the task of the therapist to choose words and gestures which, when combined within the head of the patient, will produce something that is alive. Unlike the scientific expert who chooses his words in such a way that the dictionary definition corresponds to the state of affairs to be described,

the therapist cares for the impact words have upon people. . . . [A task of the psychotherapist] is to produce an
effect. [p. 112]

A fundamental difference of course, between the poet's
purpose and the therapist's is that the poet communicates
his own feelings, although he hopes to strike a universal
chord and thus make a statement of those personal to the
reader too. The analyst, for the most part—there are
instances of exception—communicates predominantly
what is within the patient, although the former most
basically knows this because it resonates within himself.

In a letter to Robert Hutchins, Edward Dahlberg
stated, "A writer should employ a language that can
pierce the heart or awaken the mind" (Seaver 1966, p.
23). So, too, many times, should the analyst. The creative
artists offer many lessons that we can apply to our work,
especially in the realm of communication. Telling it like
it is, at its best, consists of precision, perceptiveness, pith,
and profundity.

"What is the motive for metaphor in any poet—in
any poetic sensibility—but the ceaseless defining of the
self and of the world by way of language?" asks and
answers Joyce Carol Oates (1988). Since we therapists
similarly work toward "defining the self" and endeavor to
do so "by way of language," might that special
communicative mode, metaphor, equally and richly
serve us as well? It is here that we may profit from what
the poet demonstrates to us of the value of imagery—the
special value of images for concentrated effect, for pithy
communication, and as vehicles to contact affect. What
is presented in this chapter is a method of interpretation
that employs imagery in the service of achieving insight

by establishing more immediate connection with feelings.

Deutsch (1953) and Kanzer (1958) have discussed
image formation on the part of the patient during the free
associative process. This chapter addresses the other side
of the collaboration, the analyst and the images formed in
his head in response to the patient's free associations,
defenses, resistances, transference, experience, feelings,
and characterological patterns.[1]

Images the Analyst Might Share

In our search for serviceable therapeutic tools, we are
ever alert for some small interpretive innovation that can
be used to make psychoanalytic technique more effective.
Frequently we observe that our interpretations are going
in one proverbial ear of the patient and out the other.
However, an *occasional* one will strike sparks in between.
It is at such moments that we can sense the patient's
feeling of conjunction between the interpretation and
something within. To accomplish this, Strachey (1934)
says, "interpretation must be emotionally 'immediate'; the
patient must experience it as something actual." Admittedly, none of this is new. But how do we do it?

To quicken the process of assisting a patient to sense
himself at and beneath his defenses, both within himself
and in the relationship with the therapist, I have found
one emphasis particularly helpful. This emphasis is one

---

[1]Imagery is also employed in behavior therapy, but in a very different way,
tangential to our present direction of inquiry.

of striving, where possible, for conjoint vividness, and this by using images.

Communication to the patient in the form of images offers the sterling advantages of (1) economy of words, (2) directness of meaning, (3) basic pictorial expression, and (4) density of affect — the last perhaps the most important of the four.

To illustrate, I will borrow a bit from what I have expressed elsewhere (Hammer 1968), extending and integrating it with fresh material. To a masochistic patient, I once observed, "How nice to get a wound you can lick."

"Wham! That connected," he said. I was struck by the degree to which this communication was arresting — and reached the patient as previous conventional interpretive explanations had not.

Another patient, an intellectualizing, obsessive-compulsive individual, "always," in his words, "told the truth to everyone, no matter what!" I had earlier expressed to him my impression that under the guise of truth he was often actually releasing hostility. He agreed from the top of his head only. Then one day when he was telling me a story of how he had just "told the truth" to a colleague about the latter's faults, I observed, "With that one you really *hit him right on the jaw.*" At another time when he used the "truth" as a weapon, this time against his father, I commented, "That must have landed squarely *between his eyes,*" suggesting the David-and-Goliath image in addition to the aggressive one. Images have as their objective the production of an effect through multilayered communication. These images, in two consecutive sessions, succeeded in transposing the discussion of the patient's underlying anger to the interior plane on which it raged. For him, the insight was then not in the nature of something *inferred,* but of something *experienced;* it was not merely cognitive, but affective. For the first time the patient could feel the anger, which had been deflected into his intellect, closer to home, as he reported, in his "muscles" and in his "gut."

A colleague (my wife Lila) supplies another example. She commented to a female patient with symptoms of hysteria, "You seem to comfort yourself by hugging your misery like a teddy bear." Images may do service in referring in concentrated fashion to more than one element at a time — as the foregoing one did, to both the patient's childishness and her woe, which she nourished and exploited for secondary gains. Such interpretations may be used also when the therapist wishes a comment either to be sobering or to possess some element of surprise, or both. It can be compelling, in a way that few other styles can, when a therapist feels a need for a mode of expression, during sluggish phases of the treatment, to focus attention on an interpretive possibility. (At the same time, of course, the sluggish phase is investigated.)

To a young psychiatrist in analysis who was "interpreting" to his wife almost everything she did at home, I found the most effective thing I ever communicated to him about it to be: "It's important not to get so used to tearing away people's masks that you no longer hear the rip." Here, auditory *and* visual imagery were jointly employed to put the patient in touch with the raw affect of hurting others.

Auditory imagery can be as effective as visual. To a 36-year-old male patient, I commented that he seemed continually to pretend boyishness to feel safe. The patient showed no real grasp of what I meant until I added, "I hear a 'gee whiz' and a 'golly gee' between the lines when you talk." As treatment went on to address his character armor, he would refer to this defense as his "golly-gee role," and in so doing would stay in contact with its feeling as well as its meaning.

The sense of taste may also serve, as in the comment to a relentlessly Pollyannaish patient regarding his tendency to put "gobs of gooey whipped cream on everything." This same patient, I'll call him Harry, was an actor in musical comedies. If he lost a role, it was all for the best: how much more comfortable he would be in the *new* role he would get. If a play he was in closed, what an opportunity it was to go on to bigger and better ones. When he got a part, it was always going to lead to great things. To prepare him for the later inspection of his use of denial and the underlying feelings he tucked away under the Pollyannaishness, I one day added to the "whipped cream" metaphor a stronger one. "Harry," I heard myself say, in part confronting and in part reacting, "I wonder if you were up to your neck in a huge barrel of shit, if you would splash around and exclaim in glee, 'Oh, how gushy!'"

Images may provide the impact when confrontations are needed in the preparatory work of moving an ego-syntonic symptom to an ego-alien position. The patient becomes more open to the later work only as his defenses become ego alien enough for him to recognize them as an obstructing part of himself, as a problem that he would care to overcome. Once a good working alliance is established between the analyst and the patient's healthy ego, the analyst can be therapeutically effective even when his metaphors seem harsh. A patient in a good working relationship fully senses when the target is not himself but rather his symptoms.

Jeff, an isolated, obsessional young man of 20, seemed to live beside life more than in it. I put him into group therapy, and there, as in his individual sessions, he employed language more to fend off feelings than to express them. Among other things, concrete suggestions had been made to him by fellow group members: to change his job to one where there were other young people, to join clubs in order to meet girls, and so on. Over the months, he fended off one suggestion after another, just as he fended off the exploratory and the interpersonal in group. He would then pass off some trivial and insubstantial effort he had made in order to demonstrate to the group members that he was "trying." These efforts were so token in nature that one group member said, shaking Jeff both into affect and into realization, "You're spending your time looking for a Band-Aid, when what you need is a blood transfusion."

A 27-year-old patient, a gifted photographer, was unable to work professionally, although he had previously won a number of amateur awards. If he were to function, in his words, "as an adult" and charge a fee for his services, he was afraid his camera would not work, that it would not focus right, that the zoom lens wouldn't zoom, that there would be, he concluded, "some silly thing I would overlook," even though such a thing had never happened to him. The patient intermittently suffered from impotence. In his dreams, fears of bodily damage and castration were rather prominent. "You seem afraid that, while shooting, your machine will fail you," I said one day, having reached advisedly for the words *shooting* and *machine.* I paused and added, "Could it be that you make a sacrifice of the machine you hold above the waist, to attempt to preserve intact the one below?" A slow dawning came. This was followed, in later months, by a peeling away of the displacement, and he found himself then able to work professionally. The therapeutic work to resolve the impotence took longer.

I think of another patient, a man who appeared to have been unconsciously prompted to adopt a facade of effeminate and bumbling inefficiency in order to cover the seeping through of his underlying hostility. One day when both aspects, the characterological surface and the underlying feelings, were activated in a particular session, an image flashed to my mind, and I shared it: "It's of someone adopting a baby's stumbling walk . . . in order to step on people's toes with impunity." This proved to be the first effective step in the task of helping the patient, first, to identify, next, experience and, eventually, strip away the self-deceptive camouflage. Once his aggression was unmasked, there was little need to maintain the masquerade of stumbling ineffectuality.

This same patient had been born in Czechoslovakia during World War II. His Jewish family had been passing as non-Jewish with the help of gentile friends. To ensure their safety and to guard against their son's being exposed in an inspection for the presence of circumcision, they dressed him as a little girl.

One day they heard that storm troopers were on their way to the town. The Jewish families fled to the woods. During the days there, the patient developed an inflammation of his penis. It became increasingly serious, so his family decided to risk taking him to one of the towns where, people said, a doctor was friendly and might be trusted. This turned out to be so. Upon returning to the shelter in the woods, they discovered, to their horror, that in the interim the other families had been found and taken off to concentration camps. At the time, and over the years, the patient was celebrated as responsible for having saved the family from destruction.

Later, as a young adult in his mid-20s, he entered analysis for symptoms of a neurotic character disorder. Exasperated by his bungling demeanor, his wife and, subsequently, other women had broken off with him. As each relationship with a woman neared a point of success, the patient would resurrect his ineffectual style.

"Your safety need no longer depend," I said one day, reaching for a metaphor from his personal past, "as it once did with the Nazis, on wearing girl's clothes or having an injured penis."

He related to the image with that special feeling that signals an emotional connection and an affective linking of the past with the present. In the working-through that followed, the patient assimilated the insight and was able to make important differentiations—between then and now, between reality and unreality, and between the child he was and the adult he might now become.

Misuse of Images

One point of caution: We must not inundate the patient with images. This type of interpretive style should be used judiciously. Generally, our responses should be *simple*. Our pivotal roles are those of "quiet observer, listener, and occasionally commentator" (Menninger 1958, p. 129). Against this backdrop the occasional image that occurs to the analyst in reference to any single patient remains infrequent and, as such, has the additional advantages of providing a change of pace and enlivening the treatment process.

Greater caution is necessary here to be sure that the interpretations offered are valid, since the effect of suggestion on suggestible patients, I find, is greater when images are used in interpretations.

Openness and richer productivity, while valuable, are no correlate, much less criterion, of the validity of an interpretation. As Langs (1976b) points out, in his instructive paper on Freud's treatment experience with Dora, increased productivity on the part of the analysand may at times express intensified reactions to the relatively invalid communications offered by the analyst.

The View from Other Angles

Words are more distant abstractions than are pictures. Pictures are closer to the concrete, to the actual. Word pictures fall between these two communicative levels. Pezder (1985), comparing the impact of the visual versus the auditory, found that the visual carries a greater impact. The hierarchy of neurological functioning, as first suggested by Jackson (1926, 1958), confirms this view: the abstract is a more surface and later evolutionary acquisition than is the concrete. Goldstein's (1942, 1948, 1963) work with aphasics during, and since, World War II provides additional support.

The experimental area also supplies congruence. An interesting study invites our attention. Three groups of boys were engaged in a dart-throwing procedure. One group practiced throwing darts at a target, another group imagined throwing darts, and a third did neither. After this, all three groups threw darts and were judged for accuracy. The intriguing finding was that the group that imagined throwing darts fell midway between the group that actually practiced this activity and the group that neither practiced nor imagined doing it. Apparently, imagining is a midway procedure, approaching the actual (Arnold and Gasson 1954).

Supportive data come from still another direction, the physiological. Subjects who were asked to imagine various activities — for example, riding a bicycle — showed electroencephalogram patterns and physiological responses more like those of individuals actually bicycling (in place), and less like those of a control group (Arnold 1960). Thus "trying on" the image is not a passive experience, but a *participative* one. This explains the patient's report of experiencing a sensation in his muscles upon hearing the interpretation that his telling the "truth" must have hit his colleague "right smack on the jaw."

Kepes (1966) further suggests that the proper use of visual perception (like poetry) reopens the innocent eye and so, in a sense, rejuvenates the mind. In an adjacent vein, Ahsen (1968) and Kapecs (1957) speak of imagery providing access to our earliest memories, from those phases of development before language was firmly established.

"It appears that there are . . . two main encoding systems: a verbal-sequential one and an imagery-spatial parallel processing one. . . . The imagery system, due to its concrete and contextual nature, appears more akin to perception" (Sheikh 1977, p. 1). Accordingly, images possess a noteworthy ability to effect both emotional and physiological changes (Paivio 1973, Sheikh and Panagiotous 1975, Zikmund 1975). All the closer to the issues of treatment, Reyher (1963) demonstrates that free imagery is strikingly effective in eliciting material from its re-

pressed state, while Singer (1974) marshals evidence that
past events can be reproduced, and their associated affect
reexperienced, more effectively through imagery than
through corresponding verbal labels.

In a reductionist form, we might say that psychotherapy is a conversation, albeit quantitatively one-sided,
between two persons. "Essentially," says Shaffer (1947),
"they communicate, mainly by the use of words, although
other media of communication, including . . . gesture,
facial expression, and tone of voice are also present. . . .
Movement, tension, visceral and glandular changes, attitudes, postures, images . . . are among the secondary
responses evoked by the interchange of words" (p. 390).
Since the intent is to evoke such images (among other
responses) within the patient, to start with images as one
of the communications serves two overlapping purposes.
It puts the interpretive message one step closer to being
received, and it enhances the possibility of reception.

We can draw similar inferences from Freud's observations of the primary process. In speaking of such
primary processes, Maslow (1957) observes:

> Deep down, we look at the world through the eyes of wishes
> and fears and gratifications. . . . Think of the way in which
> a really young child looks at the world, looks at itself and at
> other people. . . . It has nothing to do with time and space
> or with sequence, causality, order, or with the laws of the
> physical world. [p. 5]

Maslow concludes the point by describing primary processes as "preverbal, very concrete, closer to raw experiencing and usually *visual*." Since the natural language of
the primary processes and of the raw inner experience is

preverbal and visual, therapists, when they employ the imaginal to communicate to the patient's deeper regions, speak the language.[2]

In his incisive contribution to our understanding of preconscious mental processes in general, and to regression in the service of the ego in particular, Kris (1950) points out that communication with the patient is "never exclusively regulated by the secondary process"; interpretations may "stimulate linkages between various strata of the mind which reawaken the flow of primary process connections" (p. 540). Imaged communications, by drawing upon both analyst's and patient's preconscious and creative zones and by constituting an exchange on this level, facilitate just such reawakenings and flow. In the process, we may also note that valuable by-products — expansiveness, playfulness, and imagination — are often liberated.

An image provides an extra dimension; it can be seen as well as heard. Imagery finds place for sights, sounds, and even odors and flavors. It may more easily carry the therapist's communication through the interstices of the patient's intellectual layers. The feeling below the surface can be reevoked on the surface by an accurate, focused image.[3] At this point, surface and subsur-

---

[2]A young poet patient of mine once wrote:

> Extend to me a picture of almost things
> Of things not quite expressed . . .
> Abide with me awhile
> To unlearn words.

[3]Since imagery strengthens communicative effectiveness by supplying an affective undercurrent to accompany the cognitive meaning, the impact on the patient is a little like the experience of responding to that occasional dream that Herma (1968) speaks of, in which the latent content coincides

face feelings, when congruent, move to join; *in uniting,
they make an avenue of contact through the defensive layer of
repression.*

An image whose affect is alive charges an interpretation with significance. Images contribute leverage to
the patient's reaching for the feelings inside and depend
for their evocative power on truth and on poetic style as
well.

---

with the manifest. Somewhat similarly, Arieti (1966), speaking of the use of
imagery in poetry, sees its special impact as coming in part from the
agreement between paleologic and logic: "Paleologic actually reinforces logic"
(p. 733).

5

Earthy Style

The only sin passion can commit is to be joyless.

Dorothy Sayers

More goes on behind analysts' doors than some are ready to admit.

Anna Freud

Enlightenment is a word I prefer to the word *insight*. The Italians, using the word in the cultural sense to refer to the Dark Ages giving way to the *Eluminismo,* translate the concept as *letting light into dark places* — the central aim of the psychodynamic therapies. Enlightenment, or insight, if it connects with its emotional zones, is a spark that flares up. Sometimes it enthralls; often it places the inner process it unearths into the fist of mastery.

If we are to initiate this spark, we cannot rely upon dry, clichéd modes of interpreting, nor on stale, unimaginative ways of dialoguing. I have seen too many interpretations, my own included, come to naught in the attempt to give the patient's experience its named habitation. An interpretation is offered, and it may be valid, and it may be clear, but in its usual form it may fail to engage the patient, to connect him with his feelings, or to deepen him down into the ongoing process.

The unexpected, the use of humor, an unusual choice of words, or the muscle and surprise of language might become the vehicle for effectively delivering the interpretation and thereby connecting with the patient; a turn of phrase may facilitate a sudden veering to clear a path in the brambles.

"Slang," wrote Carl Sandburg, "is language which takes off its coat, spits on its hands — and goes to work." Anthony Burgess, the novelist-linguist, advises the communicator to "hurl pithiness and color" to get through (Howard 1981).[1] Earthy language, when it connects, may awaken in the patient his passions and emotions.

Greenson (1978) moved in the same direction: "If we want to make contact with and have an impact on the patient . . . the words we use should be from the living language of the patient. . . . Intonation, tone, force, rhythm are often more important than the precise words we use . . . the preverbal . . . is apt to stir up reactions derived from the early mother–child relationships." Freud, too, had begun to recognize the importance of evocativeness in therapy, when in 1899 he remarked, "From time to time I visualize a second part of the method

---

[1]Burgess's context is the downtrodden, the innovative creators of slang, who hurl pithiness and color at poverty and oppression. Might not this pithiness and color, if mobilizable against sociological suppression, serve equally against psychic repression?

of treatment — provoking patients' feelings as well as their ideas" (Freud 1954).

Patrick Mullahy (1986), the Freud scholar, practicing psychoanalyst, and professor of English literature, used original archival research in a close-up inspection of Freud's handling of the Rat Man case. Through examination of both the case history and the process notes in the German original, he documents that the Strachey translation failed to capture two important nuances: Freud's expression of his personality in his treatment and his richly evocative use of language in this treatment.

In line with this direction already hinted at in Freud's writings, now and then a therapist may be privileged to sense an intervention sweeping over the patient with the bracing effect of pure oxygen. In the midst of a labored, sluggish stretch, we may thereby clear a stuffy head — not only the patient's but, no less, our own.

What did we do that worked? How might we bring about, with the detached, the encapsulated, the withdrawn, the depressed, or the obsessional, an uncovering of unmistakable signs of pulse? In the introduction to his *Existential Psychotherapy,* Yalom (1980) described a cooking class he attended where the instructor presented marvelous fare, but her students were not able to duplicate the special taste of her dishes. Curious about the situation, Yalom observed that after the teacher prepared a dish, an assistant carried it to the oven, but while doing so, added a little assortment of condiments and spices. In parallel, Yalom conjectured:

Formal texts, journal articles and lectures portray therapy as precise and systematic, with carefully delineated stages,

strategic technical interventions, the methodological development and resolution of transference, analysis of object
relations, and a careful, rational program of insight- offering interpretations. Yet I believe deeply that when no one
is looking, the therapist throws in the "real thing." [p. 3]

Reacting to this description, Basescu (1981) says:

I don't think that therapists throw in the "real thing"
surreptitiously most of the time. Rather, our clinical theory
has not developed sufficiently to treat it as relevant data.
Therefore, we don't have an appropriate scientific or professional language in which to talk about it anecdotally.
When it's done surreptitiously, it's probably because, as
Yalom indicates, it isn't in the books. In that case, too bad
for the books—we'll have to write new ones. [p. 34]

In response to this challenge, I will present such an
anecdote, followed by an attempt at systematic analysis.
Also, having given numerous brief examples of the value
of imagery in the last chapter, I will now describe a case
intervention in fuller depth. The case serves to illustrate,
along with the poetic, two other overlapping styles—the
earthy (the topic for this chapter) and the playful (addressed in Chapter 7).

The treatment process seeks a twofold synthesis: to
reinvest emotion with intelligence, and to reinvest understanding with feeling. The former is generally achieved
by our usual analytic technique. The latter often takes
something more, is more complex, and invites more of
the artist in the therapist to emerge.

Celebrating the Impulses

I remember hearing a poet speak about the force of the
imagination. Words, he said, could be made to soldier as

well as sing. Now this constitutes a magnificent range on which we, using words as our therapeutic tools, can, if less exaltedly, at least find footing.

I once worked with a man in his twenties, who had begun to make me wonder whether he still had the ability to feel things directly. For him, repression functioned as a deadening encrustation on live feelings. His thoughts droned on, seldom off, the track, all in even, monochromatic tones. It worked on us both like a tranquilizer. Therefore, I approached the encapsulation, inflexibility, dampened affect, and ennui from several sides — as characterological defense, as transference, and as resistance — but my interpretive efforts were responded to with little sustained amelioration. He continued to drift through his sessions, altogether a sluggish, weary-winged process. It was as if he half wanted to fortify his sense of defeat and reconciliation, his state of enervation. He recognized, at the same time, a feeling of a forever-to-be-unfulfilled wish for connectedness — with me, with others, with himself.

Gradually, slowly, over three years, progress was made. He was becoming less a tourist, and more of a participant, in his analysis. He began to relate; he met a young lady; they fell in love, married, and began life together happily — until, approximately six months later when he became sexually impotent. Sensuality at once attracted and repelled him. He felt compromised by the sick excitement of mixed feelings, and the conflict was laced through with both fear and desire.

The material suggested that he had chosen a woman like his mother, and then interacted with her in a way to bring out in her his mother's traits all the more. Experiencing her as more like his mother, he began to find that he could no longer perform sexually with her.

Among the qualities he brought out in his wife was an increasing dependence upon him. His mother, years before, had assumed a rather childlike relationship to her son; she was ineffective and socially fearful. Now his wife was the same.

One type of earlier incident is particularly meaningful. When his mother was not up to answering the doorbell if a neighbor rang to invite her for coffee or to stop in for a chat, she would hide in the closet and send her son to the door to make some excuse, often that she was not in.

At the same time his mother was quite seductive. When the patient retired to his room to kick off his shoes, lie on his bed, and watch television, his mother would come in, kick off her shoes, lie down on his bed with him, and, as they watched together, caress the top of his instep with the sole of her foot.

One day he reported a dream in which he was performing cunnilingus on a woman who, the stream of his associations revealed, reminded him of his mother. In panic, he turned his head from his position on the couch, looked at me, and implored, "Why would I dream of eating my mother?"

The question, heavy with anguish, hung in the air. There were many possible responses, and my mind flitted across them. Should I offer a psychodynamic interpretation? Was it time for a broader construction? Reassurance? Probing? Psychogenetic exploration? Support? Reflection of the question back to the patient? Generic explanation? Instead, my sense of the patient, his need, and a certain playfulness of mood on my part carbonated—and an image came to mind. It was dirty; it was joking; I hesitated. And then I ventured it: "Perhaps because she has a juicy pussy."

I half held my breath.

His face slowly broke out into a huge grin of relief! "Are you for real?" he exclaimed, and soon thereafter became jovial, carefree, and celebratory in mood. He reminded me of boys bursting out of a parochial school at 3 P.M. on a Friday. He joked, and we laughed as we worked and finished the session.

In the weeks that followed, his depressed tone lightened, and his obsessive-compulsiveness relaxed its hold on him. He became somewhat more happy, free, open, direct and cheerful; and before long, sexual potency returned. Finding a certain freedom now in sex, he allowed himself some tentative experimentation with positions and more fantasy accompaniment. He began to experience sex now as "sort of fun." The intervention had lifted the symptom, but more, it loosened the grip of his characterological pathology. Conceptually, it suggested that he had acquired a fresh *introject,* now serving an increased fullness of living and of emotional tone.

The usual analytic response, offering acceptance or understanding—relating the earlier childhood experiences to the symptom of impotence, and both in turn to the dream—might have been something on the order of an explanation. What was offered, in contrast, was a participatory engagement from the analyst—an engagement with the patient's dream and with his lust, and with the patient himself. Out of the vicarious joining, the analyst's image said, in effect, one cannot only understand having such a dream, but one can *enjoy* it, even *savor* it.

Via the existing transference relationship, what was
offered by the symbolic father was more than a sheer
acceptance of the oedipal feeling; what was extended was
an in-the-flesh celebration of it. His feeling, freighted
with guilt, could now not only be divested of such
tonnage, but past this, robustly pleasured in. The patient
was thereby (1) connected to his feelings and (2) engaged
in the father figure's welcoming of his oedipal impulses.
Both of these effects were actualized by the analyst's
couching his response in a personal, rather than merely
professional, way — in alive, vivid language, in sensual
expression, in pictorial image, and in a tone that offered
liberation. It not only said in effect, "This is okay," but it
demonstrated an empathic sense of "I really know the
attractiveness of such impulses because I can talk about
them in an enjoyable, knowing, close-up way." Only *really*
resonating to the feelings can give birth to an authentic
image. The patient senses this. He experiences the analyst's response as not out of a book, but out of his own
capacity for such appetites. The reassurance to the
patient becomes that they are fellow sinners, and perhaps
thereby not sinners at all.

Now, I would not have offered an intervention
couched so fully in the vernacular to a patient whose
superego could not tolerate hearing it so styled, nor to a
patient not significantly along the road of analysis. On
the other hand, such a patient's personality structure
would not have been ready to form so direct a dream in
the first place.

Further associative work on the dream next opened
up the equation, in the patient's mind, between mother
and wife.

Teasing out the Multiple Meanings

Let us step back to the moment of the intervention. Having outlined the event and its meaning to the patient, perhaps we can profit from a more finely anatomized study of the varied elements, of the processes activated by the sensual image, an image that carried further power by its heightened dramatic form. For the layer upon layer of awareness to be acquired, imagery packs much into a pithy moment, presses prose into epigrammatic conciseness. To unbraid the strands of multiple meanings entwined in the "juicy pussy" comment, we find in it communications to the patient about himself, his mother, the therapist, their relationship, the process, and a more ambitious goal toward which they might aim. "And all in two words?" the reader, with raised eyebrow, might well ask. Well, let's tease apart the dimensions.

Patient and His Mother

To align an image with a patient's underlying emotions, one held over another like transparencies, reveals the patient to himself—not in mere outline, as conventionally styled interpretations might, but as in a fuller, three-dimensional hologram.

The intervention demonstrated that what the patient experienced was natural. The effect of the image, distilled from the stimuli his mother presented to him, conveyed a sense of "who wouldn't feel that way"—the implication being that *she* had been coming on to him as juicy, as tempting and seductive.

It was mentioned that the patient's response to the intervention was a radiant grin of relief. The relief had in it a large element of, the only proper word is, *delight* — a word big enough for much of him which seemed suddenly to have returned. He could feel again the stirrings of desire in the weeks that followed, and, more broadly, of energy breaking through his depression.

Of additional value to my intellectualizing patient was that the use of imagery limbered his imagination and eventually evoked more colorful responses on his part, along with the use of symbolization and sublimation. It loosened his constriction. His fluids were running again. Working from this beginning and his new introject, he gained a critical resource for living.

Therapist

The patient reported his dream. From the transference angle, everything hung on the moment of, my God, what will the father do? Annihilation? Castration? Banishment? Instead, the father joked. The therapist's intervention moved the discussion from a mere dialogue about a dream the other night into an actualized feeling in the here-and-now. And he spoke in the vernacular, extending a hand to the patient to stand beside him in camaraderie, in mutuality, and on the plane of malehood.

The importance to certain patients[2] of experiencing the therapist's interest and acceptance may be equaled by experiencing also the therapist's liveliness and vitality. Thus, another advantage to the therapist's employment of images is simply that it is vitalizing to the patient. It is

---

[2]As previously mentioned, the intellectualized, the encapsulated, the depressed, the withdrawn, the obsessive-compulsive, for example.

important, at times, for the therapist to be able to approach the therapeutic process in a mood of expansiveness and playfulness. In so doing, the therapist offers the patient a model, one in whom work and play blend, an example that seriousness of purpose and liveliness of spirit can harmonize toward a common goal. In addition, the analyst's "juicy pussy" reaction, expressed in a direct, open, robust manner, was reassuring to the patient, giving him permission to be direct, open, and robust himself, more daring in his feelings against the taboos, and uncowering before the superego's raised whip of guilt.

The capacity for this attitude is liberating not only for the patient, but also, now and then, for the therapist as he struggles free of the countertransferential bog into which the depressive, masochistic, or obsessional patient tends to pull him. It is the therapist's counter to the despair in which the depressive is seeking to envelope him, and to the confirmation of bleak suffering in which the masochist seeks to trap him. With the obsessional patient, liveliness on the therapist's part maintains a working atmosphere, as therapist and patient join to scatter the stifling quality of the therapy situation, as both of them gasp to breathe fully and the patient strains to come alive again.

Relationship

Interpretive images, born from the analyst's more imaginative regions, are felt by the patient to be of the analyst and from the analyst, and are thus taken by the patient to have a rather intimate quality, drawing the two of them into fuller contact. The usual interpretation has a more or less cognitive style and is spoken from a certain percep-

tual distance. In contrast, in sharing an image of the
patient with him, the therapist steps closer. The "juicy
pussy" was a very personal statement, coming alive out of
the moment between therapist and patient.

Necessary, although not sufficient, for such a
response, is an empathic connection with the patient, a
fuller joining together. A feeling of empathy reflects a
lowering of ego boundary between two parties and an
investment of one person in the other. The patient
keenly feels this subjective involvement, and this
investment on the therapist's part, as culminating in a
rather special connection between them. The patient
experiences the therapist as having sensitively felt his
way into the patient's experience. As a consequence, the
latter feels valued, really understood. When this occurs
in the context of an established transference, the growth
in self-worth becomes all the more his.

In this lowering of ego boundaries, one participant
shares in the experience of the other as he gropes toward
gaining thus a fuller sense of another's anxiety, or
despair, or yearning, or rage, or dilemma, or arousal
that, in transitory mode, becomes his own and its very
tones personally known. In essence, then, the analyst's
ability to empathize with a patient in this way consists of
an ability to put himself partially into the patient in order
to experience him more deeply and more fully.

Fenichel (1941), inspecting empathy, breaks it down
into two phases: "(1) an identification with the other
person and (2) an awareness of one's own feelings after
the identification, and in this way an awareness of the
object's feelings."

Greenson (1960) focuses it similarly. His way of

empathically connecting is described in the course of giving a clinical example:

> At this point I changed the way I am listening to her. I shift from listening from the outside to listening from the inside. I have to let a part of me become the patient, and I have to go through her experiences as if I were the patient and to introspect what is going on in me as they occur. [p. 207]

I also join with Greenson (1971) when he talks about how to choose the words for a communication: "It must have impact and yet not be shocking."[3] But he does not illuminate the problem of how one does this.

---

[3]Was my intervention shocking? The patient's reactions conveyed that it had found that delicate balance of fleshed-out impact short of shocking.

The approach taken in this case is in the general direction already pointed to by Freud (1904), who wrote in *The Psychoanalytic Method:*

> Free associations are beyond good, evil, logic, pain, disgust, anguish or shame. Every word is welcome, and that includes, of course, dirty words. . . .Actually it is impossible to overrate the therapeutic value of these condemned words. No treatment can be thought to be over *rebus bene gesta* (having everything go well) if the patient does not allow himself to utter obscene words. Failing to do this, no success is possible. A patient who relates his sexual life in the terminology characteristic of an anatomy or physiology book is not revealing his story but rather is delivering a summary, as scientific, cold and impersonal as a medical book. Moral conscience is to be blamed; did not allow him to narrate in a warm, even hot, fashion his love life. It is the psychoanalyst's task to point this out without hesitation or mercy. For, quite often, the patient himself ignores this. He deludes himself. He naively imagines that simply speaking about sexuality is the same as living it (many psychoanalysts also have this delusion). However, it is clear that there is a great difference between *telling* and *confiding* an intimacy. [p. 121]

In the following year, reporting the psychoanalytic vicissitudes in the ground-breaking case of 18-year-old Dora, Freud (1905, p. 130) further informs us: "Sexual relationships are discussed with total freedom, the true

What happened around the "juicy pussy" intervention was that therapist and patient joined together, connected in warmth and in humor and in humanness. The image evidently carried rich loads of empathy, vividly demonstrated and readily received. It said, in effect, "I really know your feelings. You are not alone in such feelings. I know your feelings out of knowing my similar ones. And now that I know your feelings, you know mine." It thus becomes, not a general remark, but a highly personal statement of "I don't judge you, and more than accept you, I resonate to you." Acceptance is a thin experience, if we compare it to what we may call *resonance,* a decidedly more nuanced, personal, emotional attunement of close mutuality, much like a string of one violin vibrating in tune to the corresponding string plucked on another.

---

name of the sexual functions and organs is used. . . . I have not been intimidated to speak (thus) with a young woman."

But does Freud go far enough? He himself does not employ the common, familiar, meaningful, affect-toned words we all grew up with as part of our intimate experience. Instead, "in my consultations," he says, "I give both sexual acts and organs their technical names." Arango (1989) and I are in agreement. As he eloquently puts it, "Such a way of talking does not, however, arouse true feelings but only their muffled version. They are musical notes played in mute tones whereas psychoanalysis seeks the most heartfelt melodies."

Despite his ideological emancipation, Freud's handicap was that emotionally he remained a fettered child of his Victorian times. As Arango assembles the history, Freud's personal prudishness was evident in a number of instances. For example, he did not allow Martha Bernays, his 16-year-old fiancée, to read Fielding's *Tom Jones,* the English classic, thinking it inappropriate for her honest soul. When Martha had, on another occasion, mentioned that she planned to stay at the home of a friend who "had got married before the wedding," Freud forbade it, regarding the woman, on this count, as a source of moral contamination. Still much later in life, when he was 64, he was shocked when a colleague attended a psychoanalytic congress accompanied by his lover.

Process

The style of such interventions is pleasantly (usually) surprising and is experienced as novel and refreshing. Such interventions endorse the feelings and convey a wholesomeness to the impulses, thereby cleansing them of their awful guilt. A sense of simple humanness replaces the corroding wickedness. Conventional interpretations just don't take this process deeply enough into the affect.

Imagery, I have found, is engaged with noteworthy intensity. It can open the affective pathway so frequently obscured by intellectual constructs. With a dry, emotionally rarefied, detached, obsessional individual such as this patient, we might ideally reach for an image that carries about as much electricity as the form — and the patient's defensive structure — will allow. What proved so effective was the strength, intensity, and voluptuousness of the imagery and its striking multisensual quality — of vision, of touch, and of taste.

This stylistic approach also addresses one of the criticisms of more conventional interpretive approaches — that traditional interventions are often received by the patient's remaining passive, either agreeing or disagreeing, but still remaining relatively unreactive.

At the same time, the JP intervention constituted more than an interpretation; it became an act. Therein the therapist does more than comment; he reacts. Here, then, is something substantive of the analyst for the patient to introject — more muscle, both altering his superego and expanding his ego.

Another effect was to energize not only the session in question but with the tempo now quickened, the following ones. It taught the patient that the treatment enterprise, besides much else, might also be adventurous, at times even exciting.

Thus the effects on the therapeutic process were fourfold: (1) moving it from the intellectual toward the affective polarity, (2) energizing it, (3) adding interactive dimension, and (4) imparting more openness.

A last issue to be mentioned here is one that the novelist phrases more clearly than the clinician. Daphne Merkin (1988), in her insightful *Enchantment,* has her protagonist come to a keen understanding: "What I want — what I can't get — is something organic," the heroine says in one of her searching attempts to locate the source of her malaise, "What my mother (for what reason?) can't give me: potato love, natural as earth, scruffy and brown, clinging to your roots, helping you grow fit and firm."

Therapy should not repeat this error. It might, instead, in the transference deal when necessary in the "scruffy and brown," and thus provide that on which a patient might "grow fit and firm."

Goals of the Psychodynamic Therapies

One important goal of treatment is to provide the patient with an expanded self — deeper, richer, wiser, and more grown up than the self first brought to treatment.

My intervention was designed, of course, to help the patient resolve his presenting symptoms. But beyond this — *directly,* rather than indirectly — it served the goal of easing him out of his affective impoverishment, out of his having constricted himself, in Freud's words, into "a shrunken vestige" of what was once "far more extensive feelings." As analysts, our words are all too often the words of the academic: dry, emotionally arid, and prone to draw from, and hence to lead to, the head more than the gut.

Interventions target certain goals. One is to analyze the resistances and, another, the defenses. A third, I propose, might address expanding the libido. By "expanding the libido," I have in mind liberating the patient's capacity for joy, for verve, for pleasure, for fun. This does not always come about in the analytic work, where we find patients, when our work *is* successful, freed of their specific symptoms but not necessarily having found a buoyancy, a vitality, a capacity for delight, in living.

The goal must be to enlarge the patient, not to "shrink" him, as Levenson (1985) puts it. The goal, beyond symptom removal, becomes one of releasing pleasurable fantasy outlets, and at the same time works toward an expansion of libidinal capacity for enjoyment. The goal is the retention or recapture, although we get older, of the youthful capacities for laughter, wonder, search, exuberance.[4]

"Creativity is close to play and playfulness," writes Sanville (1987), "and can easily be experienced as contrary to a work ethic." The somber, heavily serious, rigid patient who needs it most may react, at first, to a therapist's imagery as to the disconcertingly unexpected, as out-of-place in the "serious" business of the psychotherapy. Some may be surprised; an occasional one, shocked. But this then becomes the beginning of the treatment of

---

[4]The treatment approach toward this goal, one of celebrating the impulses and liberating the libido, is presented in Chapter 7.

this problem, the beginning of a process to become, in Karl Menninger's phrase, "weller than well."

It then follows, by extension, that finding one's creativity should be embedded in the goals to be attained. Kohut's (1978) view, similarly, is that

> a well-conducted analysis . . . which has been brought to a proper conclusion, provides the analysand with more than the diminution or disappearance of his painful and disturbing symptoms — existing in him now is a certain psychological openness, perhaps even a spark of that playful creativeness which turns toward new situations with joyful interest and responds to them with life-affirming initiative. [p. 545]

He then weighs the other side and adds (p. 546), "Such a person may yet continue to be more easily traumatized than one who has learned to maintain a reliable yet restricting psychic equilibrium, but he will also be more perceptive and responsive than the rigidly normal."

As one becomes, via the analysis, really and insistently oneself, that self should include a vigor and a sense that, at one's best moments, life hums.

Style of Interventions, Revisited

The way of saying embodies the what of saying. "In the right key one can say anything," George Bernard Shaw (1985) wrote, "in the wrong key, nothing: the only delicate part of the job is the establishment of the key." As with many creatively witty writers, Shaw developed a personally styled key. This allowed him to utter perhaps not anything, but assuredly many "outrageous things, composed in his own tonality of bright percussive know-ingness" (Kenner 1988). For example, St. John Ervine, a fellow playwright, had just lost a leg, and Shaw extended consolation, writing him, "For a man of our profession two legs are perhaps an extravagance."

Hence, a final word about style in the case presented: Should there have been any sting to the words offered the patient in reference to his mother's vagina, it was lightened by hovering only inches from the playful, by a frolicking tone. The stark oedipal and oral material was made *acceptable* and, more important, as it then flooded over into the patient's marriage, *gutsy*. An analyst's objectivity of tone might have bypassed the opportunity for the second emotional quality. The essence of the patient's dream was caught for him by the image, its erotic energy extracted and given back to him. Poetry does not so much tell an experience as reinvoke it. So, too, does therapeutic imagery. An image may hurdle the barriers of thinking and, seen and felt, it may draw the patient into the passion of his emotions, into experiencing his own vortex.

Should a therapist ever find at hand a means of sharing humor and truth in a nutshell, multiple meanings packed into concentrated expression, so much the better. Essentially, a therapist functions, as Sullivan memorably put it, as a "participant observer"; but he is, at the same time, a thinker, an investigator, a collaborator, a discerner of nuances, an unraveler of complexities, a synthesizer, an interpreter, and—intentionally or unintentionally—in this last named, a stylist. In the clinical literature, this last is rarely discussed.

With our fellow interpreters of life, the novelist, playwright, or poet, style is inescapable. In our therapeutic exchange, it is also present, if less visible, and can, in the subtleties of the process, be no less a variable to which the patient responds. Erik Erikson once said to Robert Coles (1980), "Maybe if a few more psychoanalysts were able to sketch or paint their 'ideas,' rather than speak them in the clumsy and sometimes insulting language of our 'trade,' we would [appreciably improve our therapy]."

Erikson's suggestion to sketch or paint our "ideas" to our patients may be approximated via word paintings. If we can come up with the vivid image of the patient's experience, then the patient is asked to relate not to the words, which are always abstractions, but to the actuality itself. Words, once removed, stand for the thing. Imagery becomes almost the thing itself.

We refer to that more effective modality when we ask the rhetorical question "Do I have to draw you a picture?" *Thinking* ideas is not at all the same as *experiencing* them. Metaphors come closer than do rational explanations to the reality, the taste, of things. From the affective ingredients captured in an image, it derives its blood and fiber, putting the patient in touch with that blood and fiber within him. The image connects a patient not only with the substance but also with the texture of his yearnings, or his appetites, or his fears, or his anguish. It allows him to feel them under his ribs.

Thus we might, like Joseph Conrad, infuse new life into the "old, old words worn thin . . . by . . . careless usage," and thus to "make you feel . . . to make you see." In line with Anatole Broyard's (1988) observation of the short story, an image similarly says "this is how it is, how it feels." To speak to our patients less like an essayist and more like a poet might both shorten our inordinately lengthy treatment and deepen our work.

6

Creative Style

With different patients, imaged interventions, not unexpectedly, interact with their basic personality integrations in different characteristic ways. In comparing the hysteric, the obsessive-compulsive, and the creative, for example, we find a triangular positioning, and we may use the first two as background for a discussion of the third, the writers and artists who come for treatment.

The hysteric and the obsessive-compulsive illustrate the polarities of personality style and opposite sequences in the process of response to imagery as it moves to unite feeling and thought in the patient. The hysteric displays lavish feelings but does not know much of the meaning of what is felt. The obsessive-compulsive, it has been said, "knows everything, and feels nothing."

With the hysteric, the image sometimes becomes the vehicle of a significance that the patient does not yet grasp, but yet can at least now coherently feel. For the obsessive-compulsive, the problem is more complex, and the sequence is from thought to, next, contact with feelings. Images are mobilized to lift the patient from a condition of rigidity and ritualized interactions. Such patients breathe rarefied emotional air, are abstracted and distant. What is wanted is an occasional whiff of emotion, a word or two in session from the therapist with which to connect, a turn of phrase to catch and tease the wandering ear. In an analyst's style, what is helpful is not only the use of the liveliness of imagery but more generally a vibrance of tone, a robustness, and, ultimately, judiciously, occasionally, the goal of connecting with the patient in the genuineness of a mingling of laughter (see next chapter). One may now and then faintly lace the therapeutic process with small seasonings from these ingredients, adding a sprig of parsley or, with those who need more, a dash of horseradish. But one does so when it feels right, when it confirms something basic.

A *turn of phrase,* mentioned in the previous paragraph, succinctly makes the point, or readily conveys the meaning of a symbol, or neatly demonstrates an equation between two things. I was working with a man in his 30s who was "sent" to therapy by his wife because he had not had intercourse with her for the past two years. She was a rather dominant woman (who was also in therapy), and he was a passive man. Similarly, it turned out, his mother had been an "in-charge" mate and his father a subservient one. The usual scene when his father would return home from work was one in which, before he settled down to look at the paper before dinner, his wife would point out which of the five children had been bad, and he, without inquiry, would take those offenders upstairs one by one and hit them, methodically, without anger, and with little involvement.

My patient's refusal to have sex now reflected both his fear of, and retaliating anger at, women. Behind this, his identity problem was one of confronting a deep perplexity. To identify with the commanding, powerful parent of stature and significance was to identify with a female. To identify as a male was to identify with the secondary, servile, lesser image.

And there were other complexities. The patient's "symptom" was a demonstration that, unlike his father, who couldn't say no to his wife, the patient *could* say no to his. There was an inverse underlying meaning at work: to not "comply" with his wife was masculine; to have sex with her was unmasculine, submissive, being a flunky.

What had precipitated the patient's symptom was his wife's criticism that he was performing the sex act "like a stick," without enthusiasm, much as his father had followed his mother's requests. The turn of phrase that served to bring the essence of all this home to the patient was "As your father was subservient to his wife's command to *raise his arm* to you, you *won't raise anything* to accede to your wife." There was a pause. His eyes lit up, seeing. And on its heels, feeling. There was recognition of the equation of raised arm and penis (erection), one obedient to, and the other holding back from, the woman's request. Raising a limb was compliance; flaccidity was assertion; the former was unmasculine; the latter, paradoxically, masculine. It was an assertive thrust not to perform to his wife's requirements, as his father, lackey-like, had to his.

The artistic or creative gather as another group: patients with a ready and special reactivity to imagery. These patients are particularly responsive to imagery, as if to say *Now you're talking my language.* The creative are at a point of responsiveness that embodies a richer mix of feelings *and* thought. The imaged interpretation takes them further into, simultaneously, their affect and their understanding—compared to the hysteric and the obsessive-compulsive, into both wider and deeper regions. At the same time, the pace is more immediate, the responses more emotionally fibered, the process fuller. I think of a playwright who wrote me from Europe, where he had gone to live after completing his analysis. Something he had read reminded him of his treatment experience:

> I have rarely had so strong a sense of the physicality of words as when, in therapy, an image connected. Words are intellectual constructs, they come dry from the mind, but an image makes its impact on flesh. So far from being products of a sterile machine shop in the brain, they come with the astonishing color of pumped blood.

Patients' Need for the Words for Experience

The poet or playwright or novelist, even more than the rest of us, feels the need to verify experience and affect by way of language. For many writers—one might name Boswell, Flaubert, Proust, Woolf, and surely Nabokov and Joyce—experience itself is not authentic until it has been transcribed by way of language.

In my analytic work with writers, I have further learned something of our deep need for the precisely expressive words in which to order feelings. The writer himself expresses it best: In *Him with His Foot in His Mouth and Other Stories,* Saul Bellow (1984) creates a character, representing people in general and himself particularly, as often "crowded with masses of feeling for which there was no language." This is perhaps at no time more true than for those individuals who, when things are muddled all the more, seek psychotherapy. One of our tasks as therapists is to facilitate the sorting out, the refinement and discrimination of these "masses of feeling" through the use of language.

One of the functions of therapy is to help patients find the words for their tangled affect and confusion. In the process the therapist may have to serve for a while as a model of how to focus amorphous experience into words.

Metaphors as Signposts

With the creative, the sensitive, the bright, the imaginatively rich patient, a metaphor offered by the analyst might ideally be aimed to merely *suggest* an idea, not to provide the idea itself. Thus the comment from the analyst might constitute only a half-step toward its translation, leaving it for the patient to complete the meaning. An explanation is something a patient can receive passively, or worse, allow in one ear and out the other. A mystery, however, one balanced on the sheer edge of meaning, invites activity on the patient's part. Patients must engage the therapist's comment in order to wrestle

from it its meaning. In the process they attain momentum
to continue some distance by themselves.

One such bright, imaginative patient, a young fine
arts painter, was, during his second year in analysis,
bringing up pointedly oedipal material. He related a
dream in which he went out West with his older sister;
there they had sexual intercourse, after which they rested
and he experienced a return of sexual appetite. At this
point in the dream, the sister took him by the hand to the
edge of the Grand Canyon. "Sex with your sister," I
commented when he could offer no associations, "leads
next to the Grand Canyon of Mother Earth."

Only later, if it were needed, might I have suggested
the further translation "Mother Earth's huge crack." But
this was not required. The patient was, for one brief
moment, perplexed. Perplexity gave way to intrigue,
intrigue to a complex of emotions, including glee as the
meaning of his dream leaped forward. He began to
assimilate its underlying import with the sexual sensations of the experience of the dream's manifest content.
Rich associations and feelings followed in this and sub-
sequent sessions.

Earlier in therapy this same patient, who had lost his
mother when he was 6 years old and had gained a
stepmother when he was entering puberty, reported that
the latter, twelve years his father's junior, would walk
around the house in a slip. After recalling this memory of
his stepmother as provocative, he began the following
session by reporting a disquieting dream in which he was
unable to find a parking spot for his car. He could offer
no association other than that there were few parking
spaces to be had in New York, where he lived. I did not
raise the speculative possibility of the car in his dream as

a phallic symbol, nor the space a vaginal one, but merely inquired, offering just a hint, "No place into which to put your machine?" That connected. He laughed, with a mixture of uneasiness and greater engagement. He was then silent, took a deep breath, and confided what he had not before: that he suffered from premature ejaculation. He later moved to connect the two dreams with the symptom, meaningfully illuminating the latter with the former: the oedipal tainting of his sexual feelings leaving him no acceptable sex object, and the impotency ensuring against such transgression, and its consequences.

In reference to this case, and others as well, we may note a small truth about human nature: that which one must work for becomes more one's own when attained. With the active, curious, and introspective patient, the best interpretive style is frequently one that is not obvious, one that offers a lead here and there, one that does not yield its meanings or intentions at too casual or indifferent a hearing. And what is true for the introspective patient is doubly true for the creative patient.

Quoting Poetry and Literature

"In therapy, an insight repeated over and over . . . becomes dull and ineffective. To have impact the same thing must be said to the patient in many different ways. To learn to do this the therapist must cultivate his ability to perceive what happens in therapy in fresh ways, from a variety of angles, and not merely as a confirmation of familiar knowledge" (Angyal 1965). The offering of a line of poetry — a special verse pertinent to the patient that also matters to the analyst — a relevant joke, a parable, a

quote from literature or philosophy, an anecdote, or a
metaphor gives increased tone to an interpretive comment. Patients in group therapy, for example, pick up
this approach from the therapist or from one another and
employ it in their communication with one another. One
patient sensitively quoted Emily Dickinson, at a critical
point, to another:

> *I'm Nobody: Who are you?*
> *Are you Nobody — too?*
> *Then there's a pair of us.*

Prose wouldn't have served as well. The richness of one
patient thus reaching out and touching another provided
an experience of kinship — kinship between the two, and
also between them and other group members and Dickinson and to some degree humanity. One's condition,
while assuredly one's alone, is at the same time thus
sensed as everyman's. The lonely patient was thereby
drawn in, and moved, and, even so early in the process,
changed.

Loosening One's Grip on Rationality

From what vantage point might we function creatively as
therapists? Henry James's prerequisite for a good writer
might be considered as prerequisite for a creativity-
enabling stance for the analyst as well. James propounded
that the novelist needs to be half in life and half out of it,
sufficiently involved in life to know what it is about, but
enough outside of it to be able to see what is going on

within. The reader will see in this a striking parallel to Sullivan's (1947) advocated role of participant–observer.

After assuming this position, where do we find the insights that dawn upon us in our daily quiet wrestling with the challenge of the patient's neurosis? The richest leads tend to emerge from below our intellect, from beneath our rational, sensible, conscious layer, from that borderland zone between the conscious and the unconscious that we refer to as the preconscious. It is here where all truly creative production has its beginnings; it is this which is its womb (Barron 1963, Ekstein 1959, Freud 1949, Hammer 1961, 1968, Kris 1952, Kubie 1961, Reik 1948).

Ekstein (1959) describes the analyst's "sudden insights" in treatment as not being "acquired logically, step by step, [but as having] the quality of the unpredictable, at times the uncanny." He extends the truism: "Only he who can trust the workings of his preconscious, who can surrender ordinary, secondary-process thinking to evenly suspended attention, and who can permit himself to be influenced by thought processes which stem from more archaic levels, can do authentic psychoanalytic work."

The analyst's experience of a flash of insight is much like the experience of any creative moment: It is felt as a *passive* opening of oneself to receive that which comes (Hammer 1964). As we listen to the patient's material with "hovering attention," not only do we feel a conscious urge to reach out for its meaning and its emotional subtleties, but, when our sensibilities are tuning in, we experience it as something in the material reaching out to touch us.

Capitalizing on this truth, we will find that we function more creatively, with honed intuition more available, not when we focus our concentration, but when we relax it — when we actually *unfocus concentration.*

However, what is then heard with the "third ear" must be submitted to examination by the executive function of rationality. To employ imagery, it is essential to suspend logic temporarily. It is a precondition to suspend *momentarily* the ever-evaluative, criticizing, judging function of the mind in order to remain open to receiving uncritically the imagery, or the insight, that comes unexpectedly. Kanzer (1958) also points out that the formation of imagery is encouraged by the suspension of the secondary processes. Once formed, however, the image is delivered into the ego's grasp to be sifted, shaped, and judged. It is then that we bring our critical functions back into play to evaluate the images that occurred and to select those that make sense, those appropriate and helpful to share with the patient. Thus, what is necessary in us as analysts is an oscillating between the tender-minded and the tough-minded polarities within ourselves.

Notes Regarding My Own Efforts at Creativity in Sessions

What is the mystery, the magic, of tuning in on and receiving the inner life of another? This process, empathy, is at the center of the encounter in which we engage to enable patients to heal, to change, to grow. Empathy and creativity go hand in hand. They particularly go together in the creation of metaphor and of understanding as we grope, search, quest for the unique essence of another.

I will share with the reader the evolvement of one style of functioning: when responses seem to emerge from deep within me. If I speak from the personal, perhaps it will be more helpful. I have instructed my patients on the couch to allow their thoughts to follow their own lead, to go off on tangents, when there is a tug in such directions, to pay attention to marginal ideas, peripheral feelings, and physical sensations. And then I do likewise. I tune in to the patient, and pay attention to my own darting ideas, feelings, or sensations as they reverberate to the ongoing process in the patient. I have a reclining chair in which I lean back to listen, trying not so much to be alert as to be absorbed. My mental posture, like my physical posture, is not one of leaning forward to catch clues, but of leaning back to let the mood, the atmosphere, come to me — to hear the meaning between the lines, to listen for the music behind the words. As one gives oneself to being carried along by the affective cadence of the patient's session, one may sense its tone and subtleties.[1] By being more open, in this manner, to resonating to the patient, I find pictures forming in my creative zones; an image crystallizes, reflecting the patient's experience.

I have had the sense, at such times, that at the moments when I would pick up some image of the

---

[1]Since writing this I have come across a description of the creative process in painting that appears strikingly parallel to both free association on the part of the patient and a similar process on the part of the analyst. After an initial phase, "I look at flies, at flowers, at leaves and trees around me . . . ," Picasso (Gauther 1968) then works as follows: *"I let my mind drift at ease, just like a boat in the current* [italics added]. Sooner or later, it is caught by something. It gets precise. It takes shape. . . . My next painting motif is decided."

patient's experience, he was particularly ripe for receiving my perceptions, just as I was for receiving his. An empathic channel appeared to be established which carried his state or emotion my way via a kind of affective "wireless." This channel, in turn, carried my image back to him, as he stood open in a special kind of receptivity. It is only when a patient is actually thus *feeling* his affect connected with the problem, Freud (1937) points out in addressing the issues of "Analysis Terminable and Interminable," that insights occur, hit home, and produce change.

Earlier chapters illustrated my process of working this way, particularly via imaged interpretations. We may now consider one further example: A 28-year-old woman was describing a situation that I perceived as a wallowing in self-consoling gloom. She had convinced herself that her boyfriend had forgotten her birthday, and she settled down for an evening of despair. Suddenly the doorbell rang, and there he was with flowers and a present under his arm. Instead of a sense of relief and fulfillment, she experienced, "strangely," she said, "a feeling of deprivation."

"Why did I react that way?" she asked me, feeling at a loss. Turning the question back to her produced only perplexity. There seemed two directions to explore: one, the loss of her feeling of current justification for anger, and two, the disruption of her self-consoling masochistic feeling. The second seemed closer to awareness, and I chose to address that aspect. But how could I most effectively express my understanding of her reaction? Listening, I had felt an empathic link, which formed an image at the back of my mind, and I shared it. "Could it be," I inquired, "that you had prepared 'a warm bath' of unhappiness to soak in for the evening, and Bill inter-rupted before you could get into the tub?" That served to draw out, and connect her with, the subjective undercur-rent of her experience. She then knew, and felt, its emotional texture.

Simultaneously, it served another goal. Patients who are new to the treatment enterprise need a response from the therapist to their unvoiced question, "Do you really know how I feel?" Patients doubt whether they will ever be able to figuratively take the therapist by the hand and say, "Here is where I stand. This is how I feel. Do you hear my heartbeat, or my silent laughter; can you sense my fear, or the tears behind my eyes?" An empathic image, formed within the therapist and shared with the patient, serves as one form of demonstration in response to this need. It facilitates movement toward an empathe-tically necessary uniqueness each treatment encounter must become, if it is to be anything at all.[2]

An affectively fibered, discrete image of the patient's inner reality initiates a two-way movement. It helps the patient connect with the therapist as the latter offers a vivid communication, and it helps the patient toward an intrinsic sense of himself. Thus, it furthers the patient's extending in two directions: interpersonally, back to the therapist reaching out to him, and intrapsychically, reaching down into his own feelings. The effect is to enable him to emerge from constriction—to stretch, to experience himself simultaneously more outwardly and more inwardly—in essence, to expand.

---

[2]My analyst relates to me as I am, not as people in analysis are. As Fink (1986) puts it, metaphors express a "shared, secret language through which *this* therapist knows *this* patient."

"Free association, of course, by encouraging the relative suspension of secondary-process thought, promotes the substitution of imagery for ideas" (Shapiro 1970). Many patients take quite some time to become creative enough to supply their own imagery. In moving them toward this degree of liberation, it is, as we noted before, helpful for the therapist to share his imagery regarding the patient. As therapists, we search for the curious, the exploratory, the questing side of the patient. In so doing, we seek to connect with the patient's creative side and to help it to emerge.

There is another consideration. Our images, although they are formed in resonance to the patient's experience, can at the same time draw upon our own intrapsychic state and fantasies, including countertransference and induced countertransference ingredients. The more loosely or intuitively we function, the more we might be advised to guard, simultaneously, against any coloring of our communications by our own needs or problems. In an imaged interpretation, the art and science of the psychoanalyst at work meet and, it is hoped, blend. As previously discussed, the empathy, the daring, the sensitivity, and the creativity of the artist side must be balanced by the objectivity, the rigor, and the discipline of the scientist side.

But creativity takes its first steps in the *relaxation of one's rationality:* The creative analyst feels exhilarated rather than threatened, receptive rather than anxious, at the hint of an appearance of the unexpected, at the peaking of something that may challenge his understanding, that may not fit the theory neatly. It is this that makes each analysis a fresh experience, not a stale rehash, for the therapist; it is this which makes the analysis an authentic encounter for the patient; and thus it is an adventure together.

A second factor grows from the first. If we orient ourselves to think, feel, and respond via that deeper, more personal channel of images — closer to the language of dream images recognized early in the history of analysis as the "royal road to the unconscious" — we may find our creative responsiveness more liberated and our intuition more active for the work of the session. We may thereby enliven our reactivity not only along the pithy, affect-enriched modality of images, but also along other dimensions of intervention involving more nuanced and more diversified responses.

7

Playful Style

I think; therefore I laugh.

John Allen Paulos
Professor of Mathematics
Temple University

Patients often enter therapy disheartened, crippled with guilt, or suffering emotional impoverishment, with shaky hope and fragile dignity. In addition to their personal neuroses, patients suffer from the general human condition: intermittent loneliness and life's blows and disappointments; the sense that everything is changing too fast, that the span of one's life is no longer proportionate to the rushing experiences, that the world appears to be hurtling toward catastrophe. As therapists, we approach this in different ways. Among them, as a counter to all this, we might at times be playfully inventive as we endeavor to make raids on the human difficulties presented to us daily in our work. To engage in our profession, if we are to endure and our patients are to profit, takes, along with hard, sober work, a certain balancing freshness — liveliness — of spirit.

A congruence emerges in two observations from different vantage points. The creative writer and the psychoanalyst offer overlapping discernments. Of humor, E. B. White wrote, "It plays close to the flame which is Truth and sometimes the reader feels the heat" — or in the clinical parallel, it could be extended, the patient feels the heat, at other times its inviting warmth. Similarly, one type of humor, wit, was defined by Freud (1905) as a "quick, vivid illumination of the truth" — putting this mode squarely among the serviceable armamentarium of the therapist.

Even the less pointed type of humor, a joke, is, as Arieti (1976) observes, "an attempt to restate an old truth in a new way or to show a new aspect of a situation. . . . In addition to producing enjoyment, a joke conveys a message." Similarly, an old Jewish saying informs us, "A joke is already more than a half-truth."[1]

At least as far back as Darwin (1872), humor has been recognized as embodying a fundamental release of usually pent-up emotion. A joke lifts a corner of repression, and it is this that feeds the attained pleasure. At the moment we laugh, the superego is unseated, and thereby what is experienced gives a feeling of relief.

Humor's element of cheerfulness turns away fear.

---

[1]With some, usually creative, individuals — George Bernard Shaw, for example — their original thoughts flash to mind first in the form of a joke (Holroyd 1988).

The child who can respond to play therapy and begin to laugh at a representation of his stern mother or teacher, or intimidating father, or dog that had bitten him, or bogeyman, has begun to allay his phobic feeling and sets the stage thereby for the further therapeutic work. Another dividend, as illustrated in Chapter 5, is the camaraderie built between people sharing a joke. To laugh together, to cry together, is to join together.

Humor can also allow the expression of the otherwise unspeakable, and thereby offers practical therapeutic advantage. Humor is tailored "to get by the patient's defenses and be heard when a direct approach might elicit resentment, denial" (Sands 1984), or other counterforces. Via humor, we can provide an atmosphere of play in which patients feel protected from their conflictual impulses and primitive affects. In this ambience, patients may more easily make authentic and affective connections.[2] Ehrenberg (1989) concurs: play in therapy gives the patient a safer place to discover and understand impulses that "might have been too threatening to experience before. . . . Lightness and play can open up therapy to new dimensions of expressiveness and openness and creativity."

In Freud's (1905) *Jokes and Their Relationship to the Unconscious,* we find Jean Paul, the novelist, quoted: "Freedom produces jokes and jokes produce freedom." From this broader observation, we may draw specificity to the therapy dialogue.

---

[2]In his personal life Freud enjoyed telling jokes, particularly when illustrating a point; according to Schur (1972), he "used this method in his treatment as well" (p. 449).

Therapeutic Goal

The capacity for humor is also an ingredient, as elaborated in Chapter 2 and illustrated in Chapter 5, of that fullness of personality that the patient might attain via treatment. Freud (Schur 1972) observed that when a patient "could recognize the humorous aspect of a situation, accept a joke or make one himself about it, this indicated a shift toward the dominance of the ego." Thus when a previously humorless patient gains the capacity to first recognize, and then innovate, humor, it tends to signify the attainment of increased adaptive qualities and a higher order of personality integration.

All other things being equal, the capacity for humor improves the prognosis. Not only are these patients further along on the continuum of psychological health but, secondarily, because they are more integrated, they make better partners in the enterprise, and less stilted or grim ones as well. And in a lighter atmosphere, both therapist and patient function more ably.

The Processes in Psychoanalytic Healing

To understand a special point I wish to propose, it is necessary first to outline the standard conception of the psychoanalytic process. The transference colors the analyst to be experienced from "rather like," all the way, in some patients of lessened ego strength, to "just like," the parent. Once this former settles in, deeply corrective emotional experiences become possible. By not being the negative parental image that shaped the patient's development—whether haughty, critical, domineering, seductive, unreliable, rejecting, intimidating, manipulative, indifferent, narcissistic, cruel, devious, or punitive — the analyst is eventually incorporated as a more wholesome parental figure. The superego is thereby made more understanding and tolerant. There are two components to this process: the traditionally viewed *displacement* of the sense of the parent onto the analyst, then reinforced by a second phenomenon, the *externalization* of the introject within the patient onto the analyst. Then, these two congruent, superimposed pictures — one swept off the parent of the past onto the analyst, and the other, the now-externalized introject from within put onto the analyst (reversing the earlier process of introjection) — mutually embody the transference experience. The introject, now externalized, is, altered over the long run of analysis by the therapist's countering the ascribed traits of haughtiness by being modest and genuine, criticality by being tolerant, dominance by respecting the patient's efforts toward autonomy, rejection by accepting and caring, indifference by maintaining interest, deviousness by being straightforward, and so on. The introject is thereby swept clean of its negative aspects and, when finally reintrojected from off the analyst, brings about a more flexible, humane superego. Thus health is attained for the patient, to use Loewald's (1960) metaphor, by "chiseling away the transference distortions," allowing the introjection of the new, undistorted figure.

But the unconscious further complicates the state of affairs. As Ernest Jones (1953) once lamented, the Oedipus complex turns even the most benign father into a monster in the child's eyes. Strachey (1934), drawing in part on Melanie Klein, underscores the child's aggressive impulses toward his parents, which, via the cycle of

introjection and projection, produce an inflated view of
them as intimidating and punishing. As a consequence,
children, having felt hostility toward the parents, are now
likely to experience the internalized parent as more
tyrannical toward their ego than the parent actually was.
This aggression projected onto the parent leads, next, to
taking in an exaggeratedly angry, destructive, and difficult superego figure. The patient is caught in a vicious
cycle.

But this cycle is reversible. As the patient is helped to
feel less vulnerable to his punitive superego, he experiences less aggression to then be projected onto the
analyst. When this new object is later introjected, a
benign cycle replaces the earlier vicious one.

At the same time, another aspect of the therapeutic
modification of the personality takes place: a strength-
ening of the ego. This also is brought about in two ways.
First, as the ego, accompanied by the analyst-guide,
traverses a forest inhabited by the demons of the patient's
own nature, by malignant introjects, by the unknown
conflicts and repressed threatening impulses, awareness
and healthier accommodation now replace neurotic defenses. The ego is strengthened by facing, and learning
how to further face, its previously unknown terrors. A
sustaining, growing sense of *mastery* is thus acquired.

The second ego-strengthening process is identification with the analyst. This includes identification with,
optimally, the analyst's inquiring nature, steadfast being-
thereness, curiosity, adherence to the truth, straightfor-
wardness, reliability, easy assertiveness, honesty, tenderness, kindness, forthrightness, persistence, integrity, and
willingness to look at the uncomfortable feedback about
himself sometimes extended, sometimes hurled, at him
by the patient.

This identification-introjection dividend is illustrated by a patient, a young psychiatrist in his first position following residency. When he had been at the hospital for a year, he asked for a raise. The administrator countered with a comment to the effect that my patient, not being married, should find his present salary sufficient. The patient told me, "I asked myself, 'What would Hammer say?' and then found myself saying, 'I'm not asking because I need it. I'm asking because I deserve it.' And do you know, I got it."

I don't know if that is what I actually would have said in the situation. I certainly hope I might have so quickly, and on the spot, mobilized the resourcefulness that my patient did. The anecdote, however, illustrates the positive identification and introjection taking place upon which the patient drew. By the time these processes and the analysis are completed, the aspects of me experienced by the patient in his rerun of the developmental process are fully incorporated as part of his "me-ness," no longer seen as "Hammer-ness."

Giovacchini (1967) summarizes the classic psychoanalytic view: "The inquiring, consistent and calm attitude of the therapist is 'introjected' into the patient, enabling the development of an observing ego that can deal with negative introjects." Thus, the analytic process teaches how to be "cool" in the face of difficulties, but not, necessarily, to live with passion.

Hence, for the well-rounded yields of this introjection process, does the analyst often also offer the desirable capacities for exuberance, joy, delight, buoyance, playfulness, verve? It is to this issue that we will periodically return. What Huxley accomplished for Darwin, Ernest Jones provided for Freud, but at a price, as his English translation became "the greatly purified and

scientized version of Freud's very different German,"
Havens (1988), the distinguished Harvard Medical
School psychiatrist, points out. In the process, two alter-
ations of voice were introduced. The first was a "toning
down of some of Freud's positions" (Timms and Segal
1988). The second, the process of translation, simplified
Freud's often complex "poetic, ambiguous, ironic, many-
voiced prose . . . (and) achieved it a canon of standard
terms" (Havens 1988).

Freud, according to both these sources, had never
been altogether at home with Jones's vocabulary. But
compared with English and other psychoanalysis, the
American brand has been perhaps the "most severely
standard of all, in part because of its dominance by the
medical establishment" (Havens 1988). Both within the
field and in the broader arena, in spite of this trampling,
however, Freud's imaginative freshness maintained itself
as the thrust that added to his contributions, enthralling
the most inquiring thinkers. Both the passion in Freud's
writing and our sense of the passion maintained in his
therapy technique steadily diminished as it was filtered
through the "climate of standard teaching and thinking"
(Havens 1988). It is to this passion that we must turn as
scholars and as practitioners, and it is this passion we
must return to the lives of our patients.

Humor in Therapy

To address the value of humor in therapy in general, we
may first draw upon its recently demonstrated effect in
medicine. Norman Cousins (1979), author of the celebrated *Anatomy of an Illness: The Healing Power of Humor,*

gave a personal account of recovery that initiated a wave of interest in and research on the healing power of humor. The initial story is well known. Cousins, hospitalized with what was believed to be a terminal illness, prescribed for himself a conscientious program of Marx brothers films, W. C. Fields films, and humorous books. He thereby healed himself, despite the dismal medical prognosis.

Research (Brody 1988, Holt 1983, Padus 1986) has since demonstrated that laughter increases respiratory activity, oxygen exchange, and heart rate. It stimulates the production and release of endorphins, the body's natural painkillers, and, important for our field, is effective in reducing the amplitude of depression. Medical studies (Justice 1988, Padus 1986) have further shown that laughter stimulates the production of catecholamines, the alertness hormones. Laughter also enhances the effectiveness of the immune system. The diaphragm, thorax, abdomen, heart, lungs, and liver are "given a massage" during laughter, and muscular tension substantially and demonstrably decreases.

In addition to this host of impressive direct benefits, there are also significant indirect ones (Brody 1988, Wellness Letter 1988) for our work, work that may be conducted more effectively in an atmosphere of playfulness and humor, in which both creativity and problem-solving are facilitated.

Torrance conducted a study (Wellness Letter 1988) in which groups of students were asked to solve a problem requiring ingenuity. Given matches, a box of thumb-tacks, and a candle, they were asked to attach the candle to a corkboard wall so that it did not drip wax on the floor when lighted. The solution some devised was to use the tacks to attach the thumbtack box to the wall so that it would function as a candle-holder. The bottom line is that those students who watched a comic film just before taking the test succeeded fully three times more often in solving the problem than did those who watched an educational film. The conclusion is that a person in an expansive mood is more able to combine ideas in new ways, that is, to react creatively to a challenging or novel task.

So it becomes a plausible hypothesis, the experimental evidence leads us to speculate, that exercising the overlapping functions in any one of the closely adjacent areas of humor or creativity or insight readies them for use in any of the other two activities. (Here is an area for further research.) Playfulness, central to humor, involves turning things over, turning them around, looking at them from new, unexpected angles. So does creativity, and so does the process leading to insight.

Humorist Elayne Boosler (1988) noted that "*comedy flays the truth* and spurts twisted logic" (italics added). Of creativity, Sir Isaac Newton said that his work was no more nor less than that of a boy finding and playing with an interesting pebble on the beach. Here the comedian reaches across to deal with the conventional province of science, truth; the scientist crosses the line between them to deal with play.

What do we experience when we exercise wit? What I sense is a certain iconoclastic jab, an irreverence toward the subject or target of the wit, usually toward the established view. And in turning a truth around, we sometimes find a deeper truth. It might be the courage or the satisfaction of exercising this constructive negativism, this sublimated oppositionalness, that adds to what delights us in wit, or that rewards us in an insight or in a creative idea.

The Joy of Therapy, a Serious Issue

In his early work Freud used the metaphor of a battlefield for the analytic situation, but by 1914 we find him referring to it as a playground. In operational terms, of course, it is sometimes one and sometimes the other, and moderation and balance are necessary; an excess of frivolity may be deleterious to the therapeutic process, second only to an excess of solemnity. Self-knowledge and, ultimately, self-acceptance may turn out to be something much lighter than one would imagine—lighter and, in the end, more joyful.

Whereas Milan Kundera wrote *The Unbearable Lightness of Being* (1984), it is Italo Calvino who is the champion of lightness in literature. In his *Six Memos for the Next Millennium* (1988), he summarizes: "After forty years of writing fiction . . . my working method has involved the subtraction of weight. I have tried to remove weight, sometimes from people . . . above all, I have tried to remove weight from language."

These two aims might also serve, respectively, as a treatment goal, and as one of our working methods. I recall a young patient who carried on his shoulders veritable boulders of superego and ego ideal. Although only 17, he was the most solemn person I had ever treated. Duty and obligation were all that life was about, and adolescent irresponsibility, frivolity, and prankishness were unknown to him. After two years of collaboration, I could count on the fingers of one hand the number of times I had seen him smile. Overconceptualized, constricted, joyless, he took his rigid patterns of existence as life.

The two most effective interventions of our enterprise together, one at the six-month point and the second two years later, were far from traditional ones. He was struggling — and with him this word gains full magnitude — with issues of sexuality, namely, of erotic responsiveness to the girls in his class, and of masturbatory impulses, which he masterfully subdued and buried. All of my interventions to that point, whether I offered acceptance, interpretation, or education, had come to little. What proved liberating was, in response to some sexual questions he had asked, my giving him an issue of *Playboy* that contained an article relevant to his questions. It was this intervention, with the sexual tones of word and picture in the magazine, occurring in the context of our advancing transference relationship, that advanced the treatment. The patient's inhibitions were reduced across the sexual scene, and he soon succeeded at masturbating. He also freed himself to discuss other superego-condemned feelings, such as anger and ambition. He next joined some schoolmates for recreational activities, trying with them for the first time both bowling and, somewhat more difficult for his conscience, a visit to a pool hall. The therapeutic act of giving him the magazine apparently accomplished what my words had not. By giving him the magazine, I had given him license as well, license to enter across the previously tabooed frontier into what he saw as the "man's world," his father's domain.

The second event, after the patient had completed his freshman year at college, centered on his continual obsessing about a decision he simply could not make.

Writhing in indecisiveness, he agonized: Should he go to summer school, or should he go to summer camp (for the first time and as a counselor)? He kept insisting that summer school (which he did not need for reasons of repairing deficient grades, for he was close to being a straight A student) was in the interest of "advancing" — translatable as responsibility, duty, conscientiousness, obeisance to his superego — and that camp was in the interest of "fun." Transparent in my "neutral" role, I think it was discernible which side I was on.

Session after session he lay on the couch, obsessing: Should he go to summer school, should he go to camp, should he go to school, and round and round. We did analytic work on his need to obsess, and to obsess on this particular conflict, but still he stayed on the fence. Finally, in utter frustration with himself, he one day revealed a preference and implored me, "Help me go to camp."

What I did in response to his decision, his distress, his plea, and the obsessional atmosphere that had by now so tied us up, was to get out of my chair, come around in front of him on the couch, and pumping my arms like a cheerleader, chant, "Go *to* camp! Go *to* camp! Go *to* camp!" He giggled. His giggling built, and burst forth in the first laugh in treatment I could now count on my second hand. He went to camp, and he profited from the experience.

Had he broken out of his obsessional prison of agonizing indecisiveness because the permission was put in more vivid form, or was it that the superego figure modeled what the patient could become — more pleasure-oriented, expressive, and free? I had not only tolerated, but actively, viscerally, welcomed his impulse side and led

him in a direction he sorely needed, one of some capacity
for exultation in his life.[3] I also countered for him his
excruciatingly obsessional father and offered a model
instead of there being a time to think and, having thought
(in his case, thought and thought), a time to act. It was
this that prompted me to leave my chair and our verbal
modality to shape my intervention with physicality.

Another patient, the son of a dental surgeon, was
facing the threat of daring to acquire a medical degree,
which he unconsciously equated with forbidden rivalry
with his "scalpel-wielding" father. One of his responses to
this threat was his proposal: "You know what I will do *if*
(meaningfully, he always employed the tentative *if* rather
than *when*) I get my degree? I will take the diploma to my
father's grave, cut off a corner, and paste it to his
tombstone." The appeasing, symbolic sacrifice of a piece
of his achievement to avert the feared threat of a
retaliatory cutting off of a piece of another part of his
manhood was illuminated easily enough. But this did not
avert the reaction that next followed.

When his degree was awarded, he went into a
pseudopsychosis. He had molded a defense of camou-
flaging "craziness" behind which to tuck his achievement—a way of copping an insanity plea, as it were. His

---

[3]Humor, says Sands (1984), in an interesting comparison, can be seen as "an
intrapsychic equivalent to the social custom of a carnival or April Fool's day,
when it is permissible to act and express oneself in ways that are usually
prohibited." It may have been something similar to this which assisted my
patient, several years later, to break further through his stubborn inhibitions
and, after several abortive attempts, have intercourse for the first time, when
on a Caribbean island. One factor may have been that feeling on-leave from
the land of his superego figures carried with it leave, too, from their
prohibitions. And once this was accomplished, the prohibitions were thereby
and thereafter loosened.

schizophrenia, it was relatively clear, was more apparent than real, but feedback to this effect and about the defensive meaning of his "symptoms" did not much change things. He merely developed "more convincing" symptoms and worried all the more that he was going insane.

One session, I responded to his distress by telling him a joke. It involved a man whose wife had died. On the day following the funeral, a friend discovered him having sex with the maid. "Harry, how could you!" exclaimed the friend. "In my grief," Harry defended himself, "do I know what I am doing?"

My patient laughed. He laughed twice — once at the joke and then at the realization of its illumination of what he was doing. And he was somehow enabled to take it in and to use the insight to mobilize the courage to come out of his craziness. Making the point through a joke provided what the "straight" interpretations had not. I, who had been feared as the punitive and retaliatory father, now offered instead a response that demonstrated that I could not only see what the patient was attempting to hide, but, beyond not punishing him for it, actually chuckle with him about it.

Another patient, a psychologist who had been in therapy with me for two years, had never once mentioned anything of his practice, of his patients, or of his reactions to them. After I shared this observation with him, he ventured to reveal some sexual fantasies he had about one attractive patient in particular. As he left, he said, "You know, this was fun." How might a therapist respond? I said, simply and with a twinkle, "Sure, why shouldn't we both have fun?" The implications of my comment were the same as discussed previously. I, as the transference-enriched father figure, not only accepted his libidinal sublimations, but joined in them, and enjoyed joining in them, not only in theory, but in full actuality.

At this point our discussion fans out to take up a number of disparate subjects—this in order to show the common denominator of the playful style in an assortment of clinical situations dealing with the pleasurable or potentially pleasurable. In the following clinical situations, the analyst's playful style, adopted in the service of libidinal freeing or expansion, might be as aptly termed a *liberating style*.

Sexual Fantasies

One patient had a particular fantasy of taking turns with her husband ordering each other to engage in this or that sexual activity, and each threatening the other with the sharp snap of a towel on the bare skin if obedience was not immediately forthcoming. How might we address the dominance-submission factor or the sadomasochistic one? Another patient would spur her sexual responsiveness during intercourse by imagining herself on a table having sex with one man, while a circle of other men stood close by admiringly. How might we relate to the exhibitionistic and implied narcissistic elements? A man frequently fantasized about being a pirate who captured slave girls at sea and forced them to bend over the ship's rail, lift their skirts, and be had in turn. How might we bring the patient to connect with his needs for dominance and control? One 29-year-old patient would, in his head, take to bed a woman in her twenties along with her mother, one on each side of him, and the threesome would play out many activities in a variety of combinations and permutations.

When a patient, out of guilt, turns to us for our reaction to such fantasies, how might we best respond? In my early years of practice, I responded interpretively to one of these sexual fantasies and learned an important piece of wisdom from my patient, who commented, "We were only having fun."

"Of course," I thought, and then said. One of our goals for our patients is the growth of sublimation and of fantasy release. In line with this, we certainly do not wish to interfere with what they already possess of these resources. This does not mean that we should not keep in mind the particular impulses revealed in the fantasies. However, we must await their reappearance in places where the patient feels their pinch, in symptoms and pathological adaptations. When they appear in this context, then we begin the psychoanalytic work with them. In such context, we have the patient's motivation to assist us.

So now when patients turn uneasily to me for my response to their sexual fantasies, I may simply reply out of Gilbert and Sullivan: "Just an innocent bit of merriment."[4]

I adopt a similar orientation toward the productions

---

[4]It deserves mention that at times the fantasies are not so much sublimation as defense. If, for example, the sexual fantasy is used as an appetizer in the sexual activity, as an assist to enhance interest, from which the patient then bridges over to involvement in the actual process with the mate, then it is constructive. If, however, the patient continues to focus on the fantasy until the end of the sexual interaction, then the fantasy becomes a barrier, rather than a bridge, to intimacy. In that case, the fantasy, like writer's block (to be discussed in a moment), is an intrusion, a symptom to be rendered ego alien rather than ego syntonic.

of my writer patients. When I read a patient's novel or
poem, of which he has made me a gift, I express
appreciation for the work itself, but I do not analyze
anything of what it reveals about the creator. Should a
writer's block develop (usually a consequence of instinctual conflicts intruding into conflict-free zones of secondary-process thinking), then, of course, I step in. The task
here is to unravel the mystery of what often turns out to
be a barrier of guilt that intrudes to block emerging
impulses — impulses presenting themselves for a resolution, for creative synthesis in the play or poem or novel.
The creative work is both the artist's self-therapy and his
livelihood. They are therefore not to be tampered with,
unless tampering is required.

Defining Our Vacations

How do we define our own vacations to our patients? As
business or pleasure? As convention or holiday?[5] The best
way, of course, is to leave it for the patient to define and
to work from there. But I know a number of therapists
who feel guilty for leaving their patients for a mid-winter
vacation. The analyst's traditional August vacation seems
to be so institutionalized that it requires little by way of
justification, but we may try to pass off a winter break as
a "convention" that we must attend. Is this the best way to
handle it? Many patients would profit more from the

---

[5]While this section does not fit exactly under the chapter heading "Playful
Style," I am including it because, as the playful style is in the service of
liberating the patient's libido, of celebrating the impulses, so too are the
issues of how therapists define their own vacations — as business or
pleasure.

modeling the therapist might offer of endorsing pleasure and recreation rather than only work and responsibility. There are, on the other hand, patients — gamblers, drug users, and those with impulse disorders, for example — who would profit more from the opposite example.

To further establish, for the former group, ease with the pleasurable, I offer my patients a matching vacation policy. As I tend to take time off in addition to the summer vacation, I allow my patients, without financial obligation, equal periods away from our work, at a time of their choosing. On my return from vacation, I break with the classic analytic position and make some comment — although I am first interested in the patient's reactions to my vacation, if forthcoming — to underscore the enjoyable. I might answer one patient's greeting "Did you have a good vacation?" with "I saw some delightful cities" or "The seafood was delicious." Other choices might be "The swimming was great," "The weather was delightful," "The art was breathtaking," and so on, staying close, but not fully adhering, to the neutral, conveying nothing personal about myself other than that I allow myself, as the patient might then grow to do, the good in life.

The Legitimacy of Money

Many pursue the pleasures of money, but few admit it. "Money matters are treated by civilized people in the same way as sexual matters — with the same inconsistency, prudishness, and hypocrisy," wrote Freud (1913). Since that time, sexual matters have been considerably more liberated than have monetary ones. Patients often

reveal their private sexual issues long before their financial ones. When money is eventually mentioned in treatment, it is often in a hushed tone, with a quality of
inhibition and embarrassment. Patients hem and haw,
euphemize, and tend to talk in generalities. In fact, the
current scene has become one where sexual intimacies,
once hesitantly confided in an analyst's office or a
confessional, have become the stuff of daytime television
talk shows. But confiding financial intimacies seems to
strike usually intelligent people dumb in both senses of
that word.

At times, the therapist is not exempt. Many send
bills to their patients through the mail, rather than merely
stating the amount in face-to-face exchange at the end of
the month. One analyst I know lists only the dates of
sessions on his bills and no money amount, leaving it for
the patient to compute; money is thereby rendered an
unmentionable topic.

In his book titled, appropriately, *The Last Taboo:
Money as Symbol and Reality in Psychotherapy and Psychoanalysis,* Krueger (1986) expresses the view that if aliens from
another planet were to visit ours and, in an effort to learn
about therapy, read through our texts and attended our
training programs, it probably would never occur to them
that psychotherapy is extended for a fee. This aspect of
treatment is seldom mentioned, much less comprehen-
sively discussed in the literature or in our course work.[6]

What might the analyst contribute by his posture

---

[6]In group therapy, for example, I am struck by how much patients learn of
one another's sexual habits and preferences, one another's problems with
hostility, one another's intimate marital lives before they even begin to gain
hints about one another's incomes.

toward acceptance of the legitimacy, even the pleasure, of money? What I do is very specific. If a patient hands me a check by enclosing it in the delicacy of an envelope, then and there I open it, take the check out, and thereby touch, the "forbidden" matter. If a patient, rather than handing the check *to* me, leaves the payment on the corner of my desk, I pick it up. I then put it into my pocket, not into my desk, to make it all the more a personal receiving of his fee. If a patient holds the check or cash daintily by a corner, I receive it boldly into the center of my hand. If a patient hands me the check face down, I turn it face up and look at it. Sometimes, when working with patients who are all the more in need of a rich experience of the wholesomeness of money, I may crinkle it a little, enjoyably accepting it. I then bring the patient's attitude, as herein reflected, into analytic exploration. But the nonverbal, personal attitude I display tends to be an effective and therapeutic underside to the analytic interventions.

Particularizing the Transference

I endeavor to keep patients continually in touch with the affective tones of their transference. Thus, at times I may concentrate the process onto myself, a technique I call *particularizing the transference*. We may turn to two examples.

With a patient who continually arrived late for sessions, I offered psychodynamic and etiologic interpretations, but the tardiness continued. Then one day I asked, "Why are you so good to me?" This focused onto me that aspect I felt dominant behind his behavior—

namely, that he felt he was "getting me" by coming late. When he asked what I meant, I explained that it provided me with time to make my phone calls, read a journal article, or write. He soon stopped being "so good to me," and that gave us all the more time to further understand the meaning of his resistance as well as to explore other material.

To a man suffering a rather acute oedipally based success neurosis, I said, "If your success kills me, you will have to let me die" — offering understanding, support, and here-and-now actuality. At the same time, the statement addressed us to the very heart of his transference experience, deepening him down into its very feelings at work.

Group Therapy

A judicious and sparingly used playfulness of attitude is even more richly rewarded in the group therapy setting than in individual treatment. The group setting also gives more license to this aspect of the therapist. The effect, first on us as therapists, is to free us for more spontaneous, empathically ready, responsive, and creative use of ourselves. On the patient's side, the effects are both for the individual and for the group. The freer group atmosphere thus created helps each patient participate more interactively, more freely, more fully and openly.

For the group as a whole, it brings about an atmosphere in which the participants connect more not only with the therapist and with oneself, but also with one another. A binding network grows among the patients. Group members join in the fun, as it were, and themselves liberate more playfulness, imagination, and creativity. A group that shares in these qualities feels an attitude of greater commitment both to the group and to the growth process they come together to share. As Enright (1972) also notes, there is "a great effect on the group of . . . an overall sense of excitement and playfulness. There is a realization that fun can be profound, and profundity fun. It all helps the group move rapidly away from a heavy, problem-centered orientation toward something more rich and full."

Patients who are not initially "good" at this nevertheless tend to progress with the others. Seeing the process unfold before them, they are drawn in and encouraged to try the more natural themselves. The liberating force of spontaneity, of expressiveness, of imagery catches hold, and even the initially stodgy "get with it" and unbend, becoming more human and likable, and thereby gaining greater acceptance and relatedness. All are soon affected by the energy and vitality. For the uninitiated it is, at first, a beginning, a warming of one's hands before the hearth.

Atmosphere in the Therapy Room

Patients who manage to change and grow through psychoanalysis accomplish this by going through the fire. If, in the process, we can lace our empathy and being-thereness with lightness and occasional humor, judiciously chosen for the where and the when and the how, then the working-through of issues, even the grim ones, may be facilitated. This way of working has the added advantage of countering burn-out in the therapist's career.

8

Style for Specific Disorders

"Psychotherapy," Wolberg (1966) comments, "is no mining operation that depends for its yield exclusively on excavated psychic ore. It is a human interaction." Nevertheless, we often seem to overlook the implications of psychotherapy as a human enterprise. We are prone, for example, to be parochial and unrealistic in our tendency to ignore that fact that different types of patients require different styles of approach. Each case is different, to be sure, but to some degree we uncritically assume that one perspective is suitable (ruling out the borderline and schizophrenic patients) for all the neurotic ones.

All the various symptom groups are too numerous to

consider. Rather than take up the whole tree, we will touch upon select branches to illustrate the principle of shifting one's interpretive approach. Let us consider the obsessional, depressive, paranoid, masochistic, schizoid, and delinquent patients, along with certain special situations.

Obsessional Patients

Individuals who fall within the obsessional category are generally those not buoyed by a feeling of connection with life. They seem to live beside life more than in it. The therapist feels as if their vital processes run sluggishly, as if in them the sap of affect has run thin.

The obsessional individual employs language more to fend off feeling than to express it. Our communication to these patients, then, should be all the more warm, alive, concrete, and focused on the actual.

Isolated or obsessive-compulsive patients, estranged as they are from their own emotions, are best approached through emotional encounters in the treatment process and by the route of imaged interpretations described in Chapter 4. Whether through the use of such images in the interpretive communication or through direct emotional engagement, or both, the intent with the obsessional patient is to evoke an alive, rich, undiluted experience by providing an exchange that contributes to an eliciting of affect. The goal is to keep the therapy process breathing and alive.

The obsessional individual lives in a state of isolation from himself, and this inner vacuum also puts him at a distance from others. While there is considerable overlap, to be sure, the aim of emotional encounters between therapist and patient (see, for example, the section on particularizing the transference in the previous chapter and Chapter 9, "Confrontational Style") is more to establish interpersonal contact, while the use of images is more in the service of enabling the patient to establish contact with himself.

The adjunct use of group therapy in the treatment of the obsessional individual has demonstrated its value in rekindling within such patients a state of involvement and response, in assisting isolated patients over the threshold to where they can feel more a part of experience. The obsessional patient often profits from being immersed in a vibrant group process, soaked to the marrow in an atmosphere of affect.

What Appelbaum (1966) speaks of as "evocative-ness"—drawing forth, opening up—is a particular quality to strive for in working with the obsessional and the isolated. In this regard Butler (1962) classifies therapist's comments or interpretations according to three qualities of expressive style:

1. *Freshness of words and combinations.* The most highly connotative language possible seems to be poetic, metaphorical language in which much sensory imagery is used . . . the use of metaphor . . . adds vividness and color to the primary experience.

2. *Voice quality.* Is the therapist actually bringing something as a person [to the relationship], something that provides or generates new interpersonal experience for the client? . . . Is he simply present and accounted for . . . is he actually removing something from the situation through dullness, weakness, or through empty and forced attempts to be something which at that moment he isn't?

3. *Functional level of responses.* How much are the therapist's remarks directed at the meaning or impact of experience?

Butler's classification is in accord with my own position that the language of psychoanalysis should be closer to poetry than to science. Because of their diluted emotional tone, with no group of patients is this more important than with the isolated or the obsessional. (We will return to a discussion of the treatment of obsessional patients later in this chapter when we bring up consideration of length of the session.)

Depressed Patients

In *The Public Happiness,* Heckscher (1987) states that the proper, vigorous connection of life can be found in relating to it as "a kind of game, a conviction that everything we do is a half-serious search [for] the elusive reality we can never quite touch. . . . If [an individual] finds a humor which serves him and keeps him whole, it will be a kind of tentativeness, a playfulness in the face of the world." Those therapists who are fortunate in having this quality will find that it can sustain and invigorate not only themselves but their patients as well.

These ingredients are of particular value with depressed and obsessive patients. Fisher (1966) asks, "Shall the therapist laugh, spoof and tell stories? Indeed, there is nothing better at moments. Opportunity for light-heartedness should not be passed over. Generally, patients need to be cheered up, to have a counter to their choking self-concern, their feeling that life is too much to bear." Greenwald (1967) speaks of what he whimsically refers to as "play therapy for adults." Fisher (1966) qualifies, "The therapist's compassion and taste for comedy desirably will intermingle."

As long as we don't give the impression that we don't appreciate how much they suffer, we need not be afraid to be mildly animated with our depressed patients, for a somber approach serves only to depress them further. Allowing ourselves gentle playfulness, some spontaneity, and prudent expression of a bit of the richness of emotional tone we possess, we can lead the way for our patients while continuing the more basic work.

In making a point with depressive patients, it may prove helpful to reach for jokes when available. One despondent young patient had finally been admitted to college after maintaining for months that she was too stupid to be accepted. She then stated, however, continuing her despairing mood, "All this proves is that *anyone* can get into college." I quoted neither the wise philosophers nor the psychoanalytic greats, but rather Marx — Groucho Marx. I told her the story of Groucho's being invited to join an exclusive country club. He immediately wired back: "I WOULD NOT JOIN ANY COUNTRY CLUB THAT WOULD HAVE ME AS A MEMBER."

The patient not only saw the point but lifted herself from her despondency to laugh. But what is more important is that she laughed *at herself.* The capacity to laugh at oneself is a step toward maturity and a stirring out of the grip of neurosis.

At other times, something else that proves helpful with depressed patients is, paradoxically, telling them just how depressed they are. They then no longer have to go on demonstrating their misery so hard. For this same reason, we might at times choose to be slow to point out progress or signs of the depressive patient's feeling better. To do so often tends to throw them in the other direction and into denial and a return to their fuller symptoms. Considerably later, however, they have to be brought around to work on facing their improvement.

When depressed patients are suicidal, we can, when indicated, be supportive by gratifying their voracious oral needs. We might offer cigarettes, gum, a cough drop, or, on a cold day, coffee. When such patients receive this in the context of the emotional warmth in which the offer is extended, it helps to sustain them through the suicidal period while the treatment proceeds.

An important qualification is to be noted. A balancing consideration in the use of humor with the depressed patient is that this emphasis must remain a secondary one, lest the more basic therapeutic work be thrown off its course. Depressed patients are immobilized by their own private furies. The basic goal, of course, is to help such patients experience the underlying rage against which their depression is so frequently a defense. If we create too jovial an atmosphere, we disconnect from them or we risk making it difficult for them to experience their anger (or conversely, we may provoke it). A balance is therefore necessary. The use of humor is effective in providing momentary relief or "first aid" now and then.

Bellak (1953), who also speaks of a "light touch" in interpretive work with depressed patients, combines this quality with the goal of helping them to get in touch with their underlying anger by employing a method he refers to as *indirect catharsis*. This consists of the therapist's putting the patient's feelings into words for him in a viable and earthy manner. "It has been helpful to use strong vernacular expressions for aggressive sentiments, for example, 'I bet you really wished the goddamsonofabitch would drop dead!' This method permits the patient vicarious gratification without his quite having to take the responsibility for these feelings" (p. 331). Simultaneously, we might add, the patient finds reassurance in hearing the therapist, as an authority, feel free to express such affect. It is frequently helpful to reassure patients that just about everyone feels this sort of intense rage at times, even toward, if not particularly toward, those whom they love.

It is important to attempt, next, to go past Bellak's suggestion, to move patients beyond the stage where they require *indirect catharsis* to one where they can eventually release their own anger. The depressed patient's movement from this earlier position to the later one is frequently over a long and difficult path. The blocks against experiencing aggression are strong in those who suffer from significant depression. Depressed patients frequently become quite dependent, while simultaneously exuding discontent and complaining that nothing is being done for them. We must keep a finger on the pulse of our countertransference reactions in order to handle any tendency to be alienated by the patient's "nagging." The usual uncovering approach must be tilted in the direction of maintaining an atmosphere that supports a positive transference for an extended period, particularly when suicidal possibilities further darken the depressive picture.

The delicacy required in balancing lightness of approach with seriousness of intent and the frequent complication of the potential for suicide create a trying situation for us as therapists, and we must be prepared to suffer disquieting anxiety, drained feelings, and strain more frequently than with most other patient groups. At the same time, however, there are few patients who suffer so acutely, and few who more urgently need professional help. A willingness to extend the length of session time when appropriate, to increase the frequency of sessions, to schedule emergency sessions if necessary, to know when not to discourage phone calls even at night, and other uses of flexibility, under the direction of our empathic feeling with the patient through suicidal crises, is the foundation upon which a successful treatment is to be built.

Paranoid and Masochistic Patients

Because paranoid and masochistic patients share the burden of overloads of guilt, there are common denominators in the approach to their treatment. Hence, we will consider both in one section. Paranoid and masochistic patients share a tendency to respond to interpretation with an attitude of "How can you say that to me!" Both hold their scars high, one accusingly, the other pleadingly. The paranoid then capitalizes on this to justify preexisting hostility and thereby gives license to his attack. The masochist uses his hurt as a subtle bill of demands for protection, sympathy, and care, and as insurance against future wounds. These reactive patterns must be dealt with, of course, if treatment is to accomplish any goals, but to trigger these mechanisms early in therapy, before a working alliance is solidified, only endangers the treatment.

With paranoid patients, the use of proverbs and

aphorisms in interpreting is preferred (Nydes 1968). Rather than employ direct or pointed statements with the paranoid patient, it is desirable for us to couch our statements in more generalized terms. This is so with the masochistic patient as well. With patients who tend to receive what we say as either an accusation or a hurt, it is often less threatening or uncomfortable for the communication to be in the form of fables, generalities, or truisms. Such couched interpretations are more easily dealt with by patients, since the aphorism or fable implies that what they may otherwise take as an assault on their own unique flaw or defect is instead part of a more universal human condition.

One patient, a television performer, was having trouble asserting himself because of his fear of "hurting others' feelings." As he discussed his wish to break off arrangements with his agent and find a better one, he responded to the support of a truism, "One can't make an omelette without breaking eggs."

Another patient reported a dream in which a gang beat up his older brother. When the therapist inquired about the patient's anger at his brother, the patient commented, "*I* didn't have him beat up." The patient was then told the following story: A woman dreams that she is a princess, and that a tall, dark, handsome slave pulls her up into a secluded tower of a castle, throws her onto the bed, takes his shirt off, and looks lustfully at her. "What are you going to do next?" she cries, her fear mingled with anticipation.

"I don't know, lady," he answers, "it's your dream." The patient understood, and he didn't feel pointedly put on the spot.

To illustrate the patient's selective or biased perceptions, for example, one might tell this story: There were once two knights who were sent through the kingdom, each on his own mission. One was to count all the flowers, and the other all the weeds. When they returned from their journeys and reported their counts, the knight who was commissioned to count the flowers was asked by the king how many weeds there were. "I noticed none, Your Majesty," he answered. Conversely, the knight who was asked to count all the weeds noticed no flowers.

When this story is related to patients' particular selective perceptions, they can face less defensively the possibility of the perception being not necessarily theirs alone. The mellowness of a reference to a fable or story reassures the paranoid or masochistic patient that the therapist is not "out to get him."

Since patients with paranoid trends tend to perceive an interpretation as an indictment, with them, it is best to employ statements introduced with a phrase something like "Most (or many) people . . . ." Illustrating the concept of employing a combination of generalities and humor, Theodor Reik (1963) would say to a patient suffering over death wishes for others, "A thought murder a day keeps the analyst away."

To convey to a patient an awareness of his use of projection, the therapist might employ the following joke: A man goes toward his neighbor's house to borrow a lawnmower, thinking how nice his friend is to extend him such favors. As he walks along, however, doubts concerning the loan begin to gnaw at him. Maybe the neighbor would rather not lend it. By the time he arrives, the doubts have given way to rage, and as the friend appears at the door the man shouts, "You know what you can do with your damn lawnmower; shove it!"

We might be cautioned against interpretive use of our observations of patients' waiting room behavior or *direct* reference to their manner of walking into the therapy room. This is particularly so with paranoid patients. Such patients feel judged, criticized, or spied upon when we use material that they have not elected to bring into the discussion.

But such material, if it's valuable, does not necessarily have to be lost. Patients can be put in touch with it by our asking how they feel when they come into the session, or how they feel when they are in the waiting room interacting for a moment with the patient who is leaving. That way they can choose whether they will express the feelings at issue. A direct observation to the patient of what we have sensed of the interaction outside the office is only likely to bring forth from the patient's arsenal of accumulated grievances an eruption of paranoid reactivity and self-defensive vindictiveness. Although such an eruption may sometimes be usable in treatment, with patients who sustain themselves on persecution it usually releases more intense irrational feelings and accusatory mechanisms than can be effectively employed for the analysis. The ever-present danger is that these patients may precipitously lunge out of therapy before their reactions can be usefully clarified; or, no less detrimentally, they may abandon the collaborative bond and instead dig in deeper and deeper into a single-minded, relentless, inflamed adversarial position.

Another danger with the more paranoid patients is that our valid inferences might be taken as confirmation of a belief that we can indeed read their minds. With these patients, it is particularly important to share an explanation of how we were led to our hunches, the basis upon which we drew our conclusions, and the steps along the way.

In the treatment of the masochistic patient, Reik (1963) would use an attitude that he said he learned from Freud—an attitude of "no pity!" or as Nydes (1965) would say, "No *rachmonis!*" Here we address the patient's strength rather than becoming unduly supportive, gentle, or protective (as the masochist attempts to arrange). The pity for which the masochist surreptitiously but relentlessly appeals must be denied. Thus, rather than satisfy that which these patients wish to derive from their suffering, we must defeat these efforts so that they are induced to address more constructive sources of satisfaction.

This is part of a general principle: If the patient's defensive strategy gains him nothing, he is more inclined to try other means. For example, the patient who must defensively joke continually during sessions in an effort to be liked, to feel lovable and entertaining, begins to feel anxious if not rewarded with the therapist's laughter. As the therapist maintains neutrality, the patient may grow angry. When his feelings are received, accepted, and responded to, when they are not punished as the patient had anticipated, he can then dare to allow still more to show. In so doing, the patient can lay aside the defensive role of the entertainer and be more himself.

Schizoid Patients

With schizoid patients, whose encapsulation shelter them from others, it is helpful to comment and react, but quite casually at first and without interpreting. This is crucial to the extended early phase of treatment.

Fromm-Reichmann (1950) cites the experience of Christopher Burney, who was held for eighteen months in solitary confinement by the Germans during World War II. Burney commented that on the few occasions when there was an opportunity for communication, he found that the muscles of his mouth became stiff and unwilling, and thoughts he wanted to express sounded within his head as if they would be ridiculous if he voiced them. "Solitude," he said, "had so far weaned me from the habit of intercourse, even the thin intercourse of speculation, that I could no longer see any relationship with another person unless it was introduced gradually by a long overture of common trivialities." Similarly, with a highly schizoid, isolated patient, to spend the beginning phase of treatment in discussing the mere surface of things is frequently the only approach that will eventually allow for more contact. Such a patient's fear must be gradually allayed by long periods spent dealing with the impersonal—the weather, television programs and movies seen, sports, clothing, the patient's hobbies, vacations, books, current events, and the like.

Fine (1968) cites the case of a schizophrenic patient, withdrawn into silent and cushioned retreat, who did not speak a word to his therapist, while the latter spent session after session talking to him. Then finally, one day, when the therapist walked out without his usual farewell, the patient spoke for the first time to say, "You didn't say goodbye." I differ with Fine's interpretation that nothing of a therapy process was moved. It seems to me that the patient *was* reached. He had developed a need for continued contact, and any diminishment of the little that was going on had suddenly become intolerable to him. And so he spoke up, for the first time, to ask that the present allotment not be curtailed further. The contact had begun to matter, but it was only because of an extended, peripheral relationship, long maintained by the therapist, that contact was established.

Only after schizoid patients are more deeply into the relationship can we slowly shift the style of relating. With the schizoid patient, hermetically sealed in a shell of detachment, we must eventually move toward the style that we will then maintain to the end—one in which we strive to be almost exquisitely personal. The aim here is to enable these patients to become increasingly aware of their own identity and reality as human beings.

With this type of patient, Deri (1968) suggests that it is helpful for analysts to couch their remarks in the words or metaphors the patient has just used. "Using the patient's words and metaphors not only facilitates recognition, but also, particularly in a schizoid patient, gives him a feeling of reality, a certification of his existence. Hearing his own words repeated by the analyst furnishes substance and reality to these words as well as to the locus of origin of these words—namely, the mental 'inside' of the patient."

Although it is essential to let any patient see that we do not regard him as a "case," this is even more vital with schizoid patients. This is one of their overriding fears in the therapy relationship. It is also most important to avoid giving any impression of probing or quizzing. These patients are apt to interpret such queries as an effort to pry into their secret fantasies or thoughts, and they are likely to respond by either withdrawing further or backing out of treatment altogether.

It is best not to use fables, proverbs, or the like with a schizoid patient, but instead to couch interpretations in a form that uniquely and personally relates to just him/her. The style of communication should be simple, specific, and individualized. The aim is to put these patients in touch with what the feeling is more than with why they feel it. This is what is necessary to reach across the desert zone that the schizoid person has established around his personality, so that we can assist the individual who somewhere feels, "I am not what you think I am. I am not what *I* think I am."

Delinquent Character Disorders

There is special difficulty in treating the patient who suffers from a character disorder. Character disorders are essentially ego syntonic in nature; and ego-syntonic symptoms, by definition, are not experienced by patients as unwelcome. Rather, what we regard as symptomatic is something that these patients feel the need to hold on to, to preserve, to save, so that in turn it might save them.

Significant change for the character-disordered patient demands more than insight. The pattern of a character disorder must be dismantled, and a healthier pattern reconstructed. The treatment approach calls for a continual and firm unmasking and bankrupting of the character-disorder pattern, to the point where the patient experiences the meaning and destructiveness (particularly toward himself) behind what he is doing. Only then can the healthier components emerge.

How is this work begun? A young man once phoned his father, who lived in another part of the country, to report that he was dying of a brain tumor. He explained that he had one year to live, and he used this picture of his limited future to extract money from his father so that he could spend this "last" year in Europe in luxurious style. When he returned a year later, he informed his father, unconvincingly, that a physician in Europe had brought about a miraculous cure, and he was happy to report that he was going to survive after all.

You may wonder what brought this patient into treatment. As far as the patient was concerned, the psychopathy was not *his* problem (it never is), but he did have marital difficulties, already apparent in his first months of marriage. If there was anything he wanted in the area of his psychopathic symptoms, it was not to resolve them but only to learn how to use them more effectively, how to accomplish his conning more smoothly with less chance of its boomeranging.

What I did with this patient was what I do with juvenile delinquents. I tried to "top" him so that he would begin to respect me within the context of his own values (see Chapter 9). Then, and only then, can the psychopathic or sociopathic patient be slowly led from his value system to the therapist's. (And let's face it, that's actually what we want to do, in spite of all that has been written about the therapist's not imposing his values on the patient.) In this case, health, honesty, facing the truth, the reality principle, and more constructive self-fulfillment are the values needed.

One might thus, following Aichorn's (1936) lead, tell a sociopathic or psychopathic character something like, "You think *you* have it made. I have a deal for life. People come and talk. I lean back in a comfortable chair. And they pay me. They don't come just for weeks, but for *years*. Unlike the average doctor or dentist, I don't even have to invest in equipment." And so on.

There are a number of such patients, when the psychopathy is partial, with whom direct confrontation can be helpful. With one openly flirtatious and frankly seductive woman, after I had pointed out the way she always threw her skirt up when she got on the couch, the thing that worked was to call her bluff: "It might be pleasant to see all of your thighs, if you lifted your skirt higher." Only the therapist who would be comfortable with the role can do this effectively, however. Such a therapist can say, with Ferenczi, as he moved to unbutton his shirt in offering a similar confrontation to a continually seductive patient, "All right, let's go." Of course, this approach is recommended only when the therapist feels reasonably sure that the patient is masquerading.

With the mildly psychopathic patient, once a relative degree of positive relationship has developed and some desire to emulate the therapist becomes established, interpretive confrontations can be employed. Confrontations are helpful at this stage with character-disordered patients in order to further the task of making the ego-syntonic symptoms ego alien (see Chapter 9).

The moving of an ego-syntonic symptom toward an ego-alien position was similarly the goal with one 20-year-old Jewish patient. She was taking drugs and dating only members of other races. The therapist expressed to her his sense that she was dating these boys not *regardless* of their being black and Hispanic but *because* of it. It was pointed out that her need to do the very opposite, without exception, of what her mother wanted her to do constituted no more freedom than would doing *exactly* what her mother wished her to do. This eventually enabled her to address her pattern in terms of its compulsive hold on her rather than as a reflection of an "idealistic" value system.

She could then see that, quite the opposite of being free of color and religious restrictions, she was actually acting on an inverse prejudice.

Special Situations and Varying Approaches

Having discussed several diagnostic groups requiring special approaches, we might now note that the special *situation* of a patient also warrants a shift in a therapist's stance. To restrict ourselves to one example of this, it may be profitable to examine the situation of the second-hand patient, the patient who has previously been to several therapists. The term *second-hand patient* is one used by Nelson (1965), and before her, she reports, by Ober-dorf. It is used here not in any pejorative sense, but rather to convey the patient's self-image. Such patients often experience themselves as unwanted, cast-off hand-me-downs, not so much *because* they have gone on from one therapist to another, but because of the opposite sequence: Often it is the depreciated, shabby image of themselves which causes them to "shop around" from one therapist to another.[1] Feeling incapable of being appreciated as persons, they "quit" therapists before they are "fired." They break off treatment before the therapist discovers how "awful and worthless" they are, only then to initiate therapy with another in the vain hope of finding someone they can feel is *all*-accepting and *all*-loving.

When beginning treatment with such patients, it is

---

[1]Many, of course, break off treatment for the more simple reason that their resistances are heightened against some threat in the analytic work, but fewer of these patients then go on to a next therapist. Others leave because of transference or countertransference difficulties not worked out.

generally most important that we clarify early their often-appearing tendency to use various degrees or combinations of an essentially paranoid-masochistic strategy. On the paranoid side, they may reject before they are rejected; they accuse and disqualify lest they be accused and disqualified. On the masochistic side, such patients may defeat themselves in order to avoid expected defeat by another, or reject themselves in order to weaken the impact of rejection before, they fear, it is dispensed to them. Or, they may amass the secondary gains of maintaining their role as "victims" (including the feeling of thus having earned the right to be taken care of, to have compensatory privileges and indulgences, to indict the enemy with their mute hurt, or to feel that this latest injustice scores yet another point of moral superiority over the "oppressors").

The second-hand patient might expend considerable effort to persuade the new therapist of the ineptness or even villainy of the previous one. They do this to convince both themselves and the current therapist that it was not they who "failed." The "mistreatment" at the hands of the former therapist may have been real, or it may be the patient's distortion, or it may actually have occurred but have been unconsciously stage-managed or engineered by the patient. Although it is admittedly a difficult task, it is important to attempt to distill the various factors in these possibilities, to try to clarify over the beginning months of the new treatment just what the earlier treatment situation was. This problem must be given interpretive priority before distortions or provocations (if such there were) bring the new therapeutic collaboration to wreck on the same rocks.

Timing, of course, is a consideration here as elsewhere. With one patient who repeatedly maligned her first therapist, her current one waited until she described a situation in which she took a rather mocking attitude toward her husband. When, in confirmation of this, the patient brought forth memories of how she had acted similarly with other men before she was married, the therapist further explored this material in terms of her attitude toward her previous therapist. The immediate intent, of course, was to safeguard the present treatment against a repeat performance; the long-range intent was to clarify and eventually resolve this pattern.

Along with investigating what went wrong in the previous therapy, it is frequently necessary to correct unrealistic expectations and to orient the patient explicitly. We might have to explain to the patient why we don't, as the previous therapist didn't, tell the patient exactly what to do—whether, for example, to move out of his parents' home, or to divorce a mate, or change jobs. The patient has to be helped to grasp the point that the more ambitious goal of therapist and patient must be to help the latter to learn to weigh, to reflect upon, to sense his needs, to unearth underground meanings and dynamics, and then on this basis to evolve decisions, rather than to be told which decision is the "right" one. With such patients, it frequently has to be stated specifically that *growth,* rather than *not making the wrong move,* is the central therapeutic purpose.

With one patient, the first treatment situation had floundered, ostensibly, on the question of missed sessions. Her former therapist had not charged her if her son was sick and she had to stay home on this account. But according to the patient, this former therapist then began to doubt her and to feel that she was lying when she began to use this reason more and more frequently for missing appointments. When I heard this in our first session, and the patient asked what my policy was, to avoid such quagmires I stated simply that I charged for all sessions. No interpretation was made at this point. The patient thanked me for the clarification and thereafter rarely missed an appointment.

Considerable opportunity should be given for catharsis regarding the experience with the previous therapist. The central temptation for the current therapist to resist is being set up by the patient as in competition with earlier therapists. The therapist may have to look inward for possible subtle signs of a desire to outshine the colleague. As the patient defines the new therapist as the "good parent," the therapist has to avoid being maneuvered into being "more giving" or indulgent than the previous therapist.

The therapist frequently experiences a tug to react in a way opposite to the manner in which the previous therapist handled the patient. That is, if the earlier therapist was said to talk too much, the current therapist tends to talk less than he ordinarily does. If the complaint was that the first therapist was "too silent," the current therapist finds himself less silent than usual. Here, *to a degree,* the feelings of the therapist are not inappropriate, and the relationship that then evolves between patient and new therapist is often more workable. What is important is that the manner of the new therapist not be such that the patient takes it as merely an extension of that of the old. Further into the middle phase of the collaboration, of course, this leaning over backward to be sure that one is different from the previous therapist must be righted. Then the previous complications must be analyzed as they slowly begin to reappear when the therapist no longer operates in an antithetical style to the earlier one.

One second-hand patient, Bergmann (1965) reports, had broken off treatment in the midst of a transference neurosis, telling her first analyst, "It was just my damn luck to find the one analyst in the whole city who is *just* the way my father was." While it is very remotely possible that he was identical to her father, the probability is that the observing functions of the patient's ego had been lost and submerged in the experiencing ego. The feeling of "I feel *as if* you are like my father" gave way to "You *are* exactly like my father." With such a patient, particularly, the new therapist has to be sure that traits that may be similar to those of the previous therapist or to those of the patient's parent are played down initially, and that their opposites, if they exist in the therapist, are brought relatively forward. This can be done only to a limited degree without seeming phoney, and usually only for a certain time. It should not be pushed past the limits of authenticity.

With patients who have hopped back and forth between other therapists and one particular therapist, it is appropriate to set firm limits. One patient returned to me, his initial therapist, for the second time, after trying two others in between. We set the rule that this would be the last time he would return, that it was a case of either settling down to finish the treatment now, or, if he later elected, leaving for good. This time, under such structuring, he was able to make a go of our collaboration.

If a patient, after an apparently long and intensive analysis with another therapist, still remains troubled, terminates with that therapist, and comes to me, with whom he is then "cured" in a relatively short time, my self-congratulations are muted by a certain reality. The reality is that the patient, often to spite the first therapist, with whom the negative transference may not have been sufficiently analyzed, has now been motivated to progress mostly *to show* him. In such instances it is wise to attempt to maintain the patient in treatment after this "cure" appears to have been attained, for it may well be that what has occurred is predominantly a variety of transference cure and will not be permanent.

Modifications of Session Length

We might consider one last type of modification here — one involving the *length* of the standard therapy session (Hammer 1965). In terms of frequency of sessions, we have inaugurated various modifications of the classic model of five or six sessions a week, but there seems to have been little experimentation with the 45- or 50-minute hour other than that of the reduction to a 30-minute hour offered by clinics or hospitals in the interest of economy. In the field of pharmaceuticals or of x-ray treatment, we find that dosage is tailored to the individual needs of the patient. In our field, however, we give the same length of session to all patients, regardless of their diagnosis, age, or other variables.

To mention but two proposed exceptions, my experience is that (1) extending the time to a 75-minute "hour" for obsessional patients and (2) reducing the time to a 30-minute "hour" for a specific type of adolescent patient tends to produce better results than does the 45- or 50-minute session. The 30-minute session was inaugu-

rated with one unreflective adolescent boy, possessed of a
relatively barren inner life, who would constantly run dry
halfway through the time. We tried splitting up his 'hour'
into two 30-minute sessions during the week. The results
were heartening. Continuity was improved, the relationship "took," and now in place of one half-usable session
there were two usable ones.

The last 15 or 20 minutes of the original session had
become a period of strained clock-watching by the patient, and an undoing of the relationship achieved (and
having to be rebuilt) in the first portion of each session.
The change moved us away from the mounting danger
that this boy would not be able to tolerate coming for the
treatment he sorely needed. Adolescents, being too old
for play techniques and frequently too young for verbal-
izing at length, are one group for whom the shortened
session frequently works more effectively.

This is not to deny that it is preferable for some
adolescent patients to remain in the longer, for them
more painful, session, using the stress period as grist for
the therapeutic process and thereby attempting to work
out the difficulty. With others, however, this becomes a
losing battle, and it may be advantageous to think of
variability in session length as one of the tools in the
therapist's armamentarium.

With obsessional adult patients, just as they begin to
break through the crust of their intellectualized, unemotional rationality — the crust developed to control and hide
the impulses and throb of life within — the standard
session ends. It takes this full session to thaw out the
obsessional patient's affectless defense and just begin to
get to the person beneath. And then we have to interrupt.
By working with this type of patient for a longer time at

each sitting (my practice is to use either a 75-minute or a double 45-minute session), we may note that the ordinarily guarded prognosis is improved.[2]

Goldfarb and Turner (1958) and Wolk (1967) report positive results when the length of sessions was altered with geriatric patients, some requiring longer sessions and some being less anxious with shorter.

Therapeutic approaches should be tailored for the personality integration of different types of patients. With the obsessive-compulsive, we might consider emotional encounters, the use of images in interpreting, evocative language and voice quality, and group therapy. With the depressive, we might use humor, oral gratification, telling the patient how depressed he is so he might ease off demonstrating it and indirect catharsis. With the paranoid and the masochistic patient, we can consider the use of fables, proverbs, and generalities, avoidance of direct interpreting of waiting room behavior, and a sharing with the paranoid patient of the steps along the way to an interpretive inference. With the schizoid patient, we might devote a long initial phase predominantly to the impersonal, and then gradually shift to the personal, the specific, and (avoiding fables and generalities) the unique in the patient, all guided by an intent to help him to get in touch with what he feels more than why he feels it. And with the psychopathic character disorders, we might use direct confrontations, interpretations designed to enable ego-syntonic symptoms to become ego-

---

[2]The possibility that the patient is manifesting treatment resistance should always first be considered and explored. If such turns out to be the case, there is certainly a question, of course, about whether altering the session time is the most effective way of handling the resistance.

alien, and simultaneously a strategy of "topping" the
patient in order to encourage identification and a desire
to emulate and learn from us.

Special situations also require modifications of approach. The situation of the second-hand patient serves
as illustration. Perhaps, too, it is time to recognize that
there is nothing sacrosanct about the 45- or 50-minute
"hour."

What is here proposed is a search for guidelines that
can orient us to which approach works best with which
type of patient or situation. Thus, we may find ourselves
better able to relate to — and in relating — to honor both
the diversity among patients and the particular dominant
psychic constellation in the individual patient.

9

Confrontational Style

Confrontation is one way of zeroing in dead center on where the patient is at, and on what he is doing. Thus, it is a particularly effective style for dealing with the problems presented by the acting-out patient.

In an earlier paper (Hammer 1966) on antisocial acting-out, I pointed out that patients suffering such symptoms often manifest a concrete orientation and a diminished capacity for fantasy and sublimatory outlets. Such patients release antisocial impulses directly because they operate on a concrete level; they lack the abstract capacity for symbolic transformation that would enable them to handle these impulses in another way. In con-

161

trast, the neurotic, having more symbolic capacities available, builds a defense of symptoms to guard against the emergence of forbidden impulses. Kubie (1953), too, points out that it is because of the capacity for symbolization that neurosis can come into being.

Most acting-out patients fall into two diagnostic categories: primarily, character disorder, and secondarily, neurosis. The neuroses involving impulsivity are treated essentially as any neurotic condition would be treated. But character disorders are a treatment challenge of another order. It is to that challenge that we will address ourselves in this chapter.

We are well aware of the ego-syntonic versus ego-alien differentiation between a character disorder and a neurosis, one where in the ego-syntonic condition the ego gets drawn into affiliating with the symptom. I suggest an additional difference.

Neurosis represents a maladaptive compromise between impulses and defenses. So does a character disorder. But the difference is that in this compromise, the acting-out character disorder expresses (more than the neuroses do) relatively more of the impulses than the defenses against them. It is nearer to raw impulse and less impulse-derivative, and because of its unvarnished gratifications, it is more difficult to treat. Drug addicts, compulsive gamblers, pedophiles, and others all enjoy their patterns. Impulsivity and acting-out tendencies spur the patient in the direction of immediacy and against both insight and delay of satisfaction.

Others, or society, suffer the pinch of an individual's character disorder. And then society retaliates—with arrests, imprisonment, rejection, and punishment. Only *then* does the individual (and only indirectly) suffer from his "symptoms."

In these patients, here-and-now action has not relinquished that part of its domain which, with maturation, is ordinarily given over to the primacy of thought. Their psychic condition is dominated by sensorimotor levels of development. They can neither mobilize much tolerance for frustration nor hold back instinct and impulse discharge.

In the acting-out character disorders the clamorous impulses and the seeking of direct gratification drown out the voice of reflection. The task in their therapy is to activate, first, motivation, and second, capacity for delay and for reflection. The goal is to help the patient to grow in the use of secondary thought processes for preliminary "trial" action. The aim is to stimulate these patients' interest in inner thought and feeling and to help them learn to attend more to the anticipatory affects and "small actions" in their heads before they bubble over into overt behavior.

Treatment Pitfalls

In a common type of defensive structure found in the character disorders, a veneer of hardness — sometimes cynicism, sometimes craftiness — is employed to mask the accumulated psychic lesions in an underlyingly traumatized person. Such patients, though there are few things for which they hunger more than acceptance, do everything they can to be disliked and rejected.

One 17-year-old patient took out a pen-knife to

whittle on the edge of my desk as he spoke. Another, a
26-year-old man, put his feet up, soles on the wall, during
a session after I had newly painted and decorated the
office. One 14-year-old patient wrote "Fuck Dr. Hammer" in chalk on my outer door, and another patient, a
woman, married, and in graduate school, scratched "Shit"
on the wall of the elevator.

How do we deal with these acts? Sometimes by
confrontation and prohibition, and sometimes by interpretation, depending on, among other considerations, the
length of time in treatment and the quality of the
relationship, the patient's readiness for insight, and the
meaning and severity of the act. The first patient was
directly and firmly told to put his knife away. *Then* we
talked about it. I asked the second patient how he felt now
about the freshly decorated office. What he was doing
dawned on him, he took his feet down, and exploration
led in the direction of his feelings that the office now
reflected a higher status on my part, and from there to his
denigrating reactivity to authority figures. With the
third-mentioned patient, I recalled that he had come to
the office accompanied by a fellow member of his
delinquent gang. My patient had been moving into
connecting with his treatment and into experiencing
warm feelings toward me. After I discovered the writing
on the door after his session, I wondered if he had not felt
called upon to make a show of bravado, of toughness to
hide the softer feelings developing toward me and to
disguise his growing acceptance of his therapy, and thus
save face with his gang-member friend. As we talked
about it in the following session, the patient sheepishly
confided that this was indeed what it was about. The
fourth-cited patient, who had previously engaged in

several similar acts against the property in my office or the apartment building, was told that my practice was an outpatient one for functioning individuals, and that if she could not muster sufficient controls I would have to disqualify my situation as suitable for her. Our work up to that point had convinced me that it was not that she *couldn't* control her actions, but that she *wouldn't*. That confrontation was effective, and she settled into the work of our treatment, a primary part of which was the gentle paring away of the layers of defiant bravado that obscured her authentic self within.

Patients with character disorders are often those who have retreated from the disappointments of insufficient parental affection into a narcissistic shell, whereby they hope to give themselves the love they feel they cannot obtain from others. For many of them, the emotional attrition they experienced in childhood has laid down a core of suspicion that warmth or interest from others is not genuine but has ulterior motives.

Those who treat such patients may well ask whether they are capable of perceiving the actual therapist. To a degree, such patients do perceive us, even from the beginning, although, to be sure, their perceptions are mostly peripheral and unsure. These patients may sense a friendly feeling from us, an interest and a caring, but are frightened of giving it credence. Caught between their perceptions and their cynical doubts, they go about testing our genuineness—our concern, perceptiveness, interest, integrity, reliability, honesty, frankness, tolerance, strength in the face of criticism, susceptibility to flattery, capacity for firmness, ability to set limits or to take a stand. And running through it all—can we be trusted?

The patient is not readily convinced and has many and varied means to put in the service of dismissing what he sees. If we are well meaning, then we are fools. If we are ethical, then we are squares. If we are kind, we are weak; if tender, sissified.

What are we to do?

I think of one patient, an ex-military officer, who early took a commanding stance to state that it was he who was in charge of the sessions. He would grandly inquire at points if I had any questions or any interpretations to make. He would announce, a moment before I would move to, when the session was up. His attitude was superior, controlling, and cynical. He knew all the answers. Modesty, caring, or consideration, although theoretically commendable, would, if practiced or felt by him, deprive him of the dominant role over others that was his due. In his sessions he was quick to criticize my ability, my sincerity, my taste in clothes, and the art in my office. He wanted me to know that he thought little of me in part and in whole.

His arrogance was muscled in his tossing an ashtray up and down as he spoke. As he verbally (and physically) strutted in so seemingly self-satisfied a way, the task before me was to hold his one-upmanship to eye level so that it could be shown, not shown up. As this was done, he then moved to a new phase, the infant under the "ballsy" front. He would try to suck excessively upon me in his requirements for my absorption, my friendship, my time, my energy, and the loan of my books. What I did was gratify little and interpret much. To have gratified more would have been to be seen by him as manipulated, weak, and a sucker. The issue of his tossing my ashtray up and down was handled simply by focus on the reality that my concern that he would break it distracted me from giving him the full attention that he wanted and to which he was entitled.

One confrontation was particularly pivotal. A few sessions after he announced that he was willing to use the couch in the treatment, he suddenly introduced the issue that he felt uncomfortable if watched as he lay there. After attempting, without much success, to explore his underlying feelings around this, I simply assured him that I could lean back in my chair and just listen without looking. After a while he came back to this with the idea that he would be more comfortable if he used the floor as his analytic "couch" so that my desk shielded him from view. To see how this would play itself out, I agreed, and he took that position. Then he wanted to take the pillows from the chairs and the couch and build a further barricade to my vision. After he did this, he then stretched out behind it and soon asked, "Can you see me?" When I replied that I could not, he then introduced the complication, "How can I believe you?"

I had gotten the feeling, by this point, that this was not predominantly a paranoid reaction so much as it was a means of testing me and testing the limits. Following on my feeling that his actions were more provocative than genuine, I merely replied, "Well, if you cannot trust me on the simple level of accepting my word as to whether I can see you, how can you trust me with the intimacies necessary for our work? If you can't trust me on this, our working together would make little sense." He got up from behind his barricade, smiled an I've-been-caught-with-my-fingers-in-the-cookie-jar look, put the pillows back where they belonged, and lay down on the couch.

Only when I had "proven" myself in the face of his onslaught was he ready to go on to a focus on what brought him to therapy—his exhibitionism, an act precipitated by his retirement from the service, and an offense for which he had been arrested and placed on probation.

Another patient, a man who suffered from impotence with his wife and who acted out perversions and Don Juanism with other women, joined with a friend at a business convention in making arrangements with a black woman they picked up to take to a hotel room for the afternoon. While he was having sex with her, she asked him to withdraw before his orgasm and pleaded that she did not want a white baby. He reassured her that he would, but then did not. She naturally became enraged.

He went downstairs for a drink in the bar while his friend had his turn, and later came up thinking to jolly her out of her mood and have another turn. When she would not be "jollied," he could not understand it.

"Put yourself in her shoes!" I oriented him. With such types of character-disorder conditions, what is required and what proves helpful is to stretch the patient's capacity to identify with the other person's needs, feelings, or situation.

One technique tailored for work with character-disordered patients whose pattern takes a delinquent direction is one introduced in the preceding chapter and which, for want of a better term, we designate "topping the patient." This refers to interventions that serve to demonstrate to the patient that it is not that we don't function antisocially because we *can't*, but because we *won't*. Early in the treatment, these patients must learn that what makes for the difference in our way of life and theirs is not that we are not as clever as they, but that we are wiser. Eissler (1985) has expressed a similar view. "The analyst might demonstrate repeatedly to the patient that the analyst's knowledge of ways and means to gratify delinquent impulses are vastly superior to the patient's" (p. 342).

Until that happens, we are disqualified as someone from whom to learn, disqualified as a potential identification figure. I recall one patient, an almost straight-A college sophomore, who, to earn money, would resort to dealing a bit in marijuana. He came in upset one day and told me he had just almost been knifed. Someone had phoned him and made arrangements for him to bring some marijuana to the hallway of an unfrequented floor of an apartment building, where they would meet under the stairs to negotiate the business. When he arrived, there were two youths there who asked to see the merchandise. My patient asked to be paid first. They answered by drawing knives and laughed at the notion that they were going to hand over any money. When he protested and began to edge out, they slashed his skin to show they meant business, and they took the marijuana.

As we explored his feelings about the incident, I was struck that the patient was not only showing no disposition to give up "dealing," but he seemed at a loss as to how to deal less dangerously. I stated that I saw that he was not even close to considering the basic issues and underlying psychological meanings, and so we should *at least* consider for the time being how he might not get killed. Rather than continue vainly, at the moment, to try to open doors for him to peer through to his psychodynamics, I shifted our discussion to how he might deal more safely next time, and shaped practical alternative methods for his consideration. He would raise objections, and I would reshape the alternative procedures to deal with *those* objections. He ended the session viewing me with a beginning respect.[1]

Such patients have to be convinced that we can function as well as they, or better, in their shoes. They must begin to entertain the idea that it is not that we *couldn't* live in the "jungle" or live by our wits, as they glamorize that they do, but that we know better ways.

The therapist in this regard functions a bit like the street social worker, who integrates with a gang, first joining them at the edge of their values. Only if we can connect with them where they are at can we begin to work at leading them out.

When I present this technique at training seminars, someone invariably asks, "But aren't you collaborating with the patient in his criminal behavior?" I, too, have raised this issue for myself in a bit of soul searching. I think, however, that if one's good-citizen, middle-class "morality" as a therapist does not allow one to take off the kid gloves for fear of dirtying one's hands, one cannot work with these patients. The therapist who remains straightlaced in language and moralistic in stance, who is squeamish or prim, will perhaps be more helped by these patients than able to help them.

To enable a patient to avoid getting knifed while

---

[1]Harold Greenwald, a key advocate of this technique, once told a patient of his, a procurer, something to the effect of, "Bill, you're such a schmuck. I live off call girls, too, but I don't get into trouble and I gain considerably. I treat them for a fat fee. I wrote a book about them, I got my doctoral thesis from it, and it was made into a movie. You end up roughed up or arrested."

delivering marijuana, when he is not yet ready to address the issues of the drug dealing itself, does not make one a cohort in the crime. By providing practical concern, it sets the stage for later therapeutic collaboration. Furthermore, it may save the patient's life. If the patient persists in behaving in the more dangerous way, when a safer modus operandi has been presented, then at least it has served to uncover the self-destructive (or whatever else it unfolds to be) dynamics, or negativistic reactivity toward authority figures, beneath for therapeutic work.

When such patients are young—adolescents or young adults—it is helpful to know their speech: "down rapping myself," "up tight," "turning on," "turning off," "my bag," the various colloquialisms of their language. As we speak their tongue and step closer to their value system, the initial thrust of the treatment should not address itself to a reversal of the deviant symptoms. Focus is at first on the more promising impetus for change in the long run, a close and positive therapeutic relationship, with the goal of some identification, ultimately, with us. But we must first become a meaningful person to these patients in order to be admitted into their lives.

Following this phase, corrective emotional experiences may be possible for these patients—experiences in which caring for us, caring for our caring for them, and our caring for them become associated with new ways of behaving. This process is facilitated by decreasing the feeling of identification distance that the patient feels toward representatives of the establishment. In such patients' developmental years, authority figures were generally equated with indifference or depreciation or punitiveness or abandonment or harshness. In our efforts to undo these feelings, I join with Wexler (1969) in this finding:

> It becomes crucial to deemphasize the therapist's role as a professional and as someone different from the patient. Joining the patient as far as possible at his level of interests and concerns — whether they be comic books, movies, TV, sex talk — in order to get closer to what is comfortable for him, to lessen his anxiety about what the outside world is going to again expect from him, becomes essential for a positive relationship. [p. 193]

In this manner, the patient's ready reactivity *against*, rather than *with*, authority representatives may be reduced to manageable proportions.

Use of Group Therapy

Group therapy is particularly helpful for the patient with a character disorder. It can provide a wider world of people against which to appraise oneself and one's pattern, an experience in which to expand one's perspective and reappraise one's values.

I think of the patient, a gambler, who defended his pattern by insisting, "But everyone gambles, all my friends are down at the track all the time." In essence, then, the one who stands as normatively out of line is I, not he.

If the neurotic's range of vision is restricted, the character-disordered individual wears blinders. But the character-disordered patient is induced to relinquish these blinders in group therapy as he is asked to try on what other people see — about him, but also about each other. His constricted aperture may be widened to take in the fuller horizon. The characterologically Pollyannish can now recognize a little of the previously avoided "negative" range of life's spectrum; the prim (whether of character disorder or neurotic integration) recognize the psycho-sexual aspects; the practical, hard-headed, nonpsychologically minded recognize the gentler feelings; the rigidly somber recognize the lightness and playfulness others allow; the shallow gain some awareness of deeper matters, and so on. From groups, patients may acquire a larger domain in which to be able, first, to see; next, to learn to function; and finally, to gain a sense of feeling at home in the more expanded terrain.

From the group, as from the therapist, one type of patient may learn to no longer lie, deceive, or "beat around the bush" and instead respect "calling a spade a spade." This must be preceded and motivated by a glimpse of what could be, if one were to live one's life with more directness, "straight," as the vernacular puts it. Perhaps the most immediate way to learn this, before sensing one's *own* potential for living, is by tuning in on (1) the analyst's sense of satisfaction in working and (as it comes through subtly) in living and, (2) the other group members' satisfaction, where their (both analyst's and group members') methods of pursuing their goals have not been as twisted out of shape as are those, generally, of individuals with character disorders.

Following a struggle against it, the patient arrives at a beginning shift in values, one that often coincides with an identification with the therapist (and often varied group members) and his more humanist outlook, one no longer dismissed as appropriate to a "square," a "fag," or a "fool."

Confrontation's Role

The initial task (and it is to this that I continually return as the fulcrum of this chapter) is to facilitate these patients' discovery that their twisted mode of living is cheating them of much in life. Their first act of courage in therapy is in being able to put aside the self-deception that, aside from a specific complaint or two, they are pretty well off as they are. With the character disorders, treatment begins with the impact of the realization, as one patient put it, that "My life is shit"—implying that gratifications are counterfeit, any real meaning is absent, and foundations are built on shaky sands of pseudo-values.

Preparing the patient for the deeper use of therapy means setting the soil with a real *need* for new answers and new experiences. This is established by crystallizing, via effective use of confrontation, a genuine dissatisfaction with the old.

Confrontation is the most central of the techniques directed at *preparing* a character-disordered patient for change. Confrontation is essentially a form of *clarification*, one that is vigorous and direct and involves affect more than just intellect.

Technically, then, what is a clarification? Ekstein (1959) defines the distinction between clarification and interpretation. *Clarification* "assists the patient to reach a higher degree of self-awareness, self-differentiation, and clarity." *Interpretation* addresses "hidden meanings of behavior patterns, and their unconscious interconnections" (p. 166). Thus, clarification sets the stage for later interpretation; it serves as a precursor of interpretation proper.

In all dynamic, uncovering therapies, the question remains the same: Who are we, and why? Although there is overlap, *confrontation* addresses itself to the "who we are," and *interpretation* to the "why."

The real person inside the character-disordered patient is deeply buried beneath thicker layers of defense. The task of therapy is to exhume him, to connect him to his authenticity, so that he can experience, under his shedding character defense, the reality of himself. A patient recently described his first step on the road to this goal: "Sometimes I jump now, if I'm in a restaurant, or on a walk, or something, as my head is becoming free for old things to slide forward. I come across something in my mind that startles . . . or hurts. But my life is returning to me."

Once confrontations have clarified the characterological problem for the patient and have elicited motivation to change, the next steps are as follows:

1. Bring to the patient's attention each instance of acting out as it appears.
2. Locate and hold up for examination the fantasies lying behind the acting out.
3. Progress thereby to where the patient can then be treated in the more standard manner employed with neurotics.

The Theory of the Technique

Laing, in his work *The Politics of the Family* (1969), continues to display his skill for deftly penetrating problems: "A simple way to get someone to do what you want is to give an order. To get someone to be what one wants him to be . . . the best way is . . . not to tell him what to be, but to tell him what he is" (p. 43). Confrontation, essentially, is just this latter technique.

In *Beyond Counseling and Therapy,* Carkhuff and Berenson (1967) note that "the therapist is the enemy of the client's self-destructive tendencies," and he must persist in attacking defenses that interfere with the client's full and direct contact with himself as an experiencing and behaving individual (p. 57).

Gertrude Blanck (1969–1970) also speaks of enabling the patient to recognize the price he inevitably pays for his behavior and attitudes.

> Analytically, confrontation has a . . . technical intent — to help the observing part of the ego "look at" the experiencing part and [in this] confront itself intrasystemically. . . . The most valuable aspect of confrontation . . . is that it is in and of itself therapeutic because it promotes the ego's capacity *via exercise of function.* . . . Structural change comes about because the ego comes to occupy a stronger position in relation to id and superego; energy is freed from deployment, resulting in more conflict-free adaptation. [p. 118]

In structural terms, to extend Blanck's view, therapy moves to produce a favorable change in the imbalance of the patient's wish-defense system. In addressing this system, more than influence the wishes-impulses, we effect desired change in the defenses — that is, the domain of the ego. This helps in terms of (1) increasing, what ego psychology designates as *binding,* and (2) the discharge mechanisms, notably developing the capacity for sublimation.

As drives are analyzed, they are both more bound and their insatiability somewhat reduced. What remains is more capable of redirection into channels of sublimation. I think of an adolescent patient who was arrested, placed on probation for a mugging, and referred for treatment. He suffered from a conduct disorder, and antisocial activities defined his pattern of behavior. Toward the end of his treatment, as the frequency of his delinquent activities was dwindling, he found a part-time job after school. It was one of special relevance to his psychic economy — as a chicken killer in a poultry market. He enjoyed the work, perhaps because his "heart was in it," and he did it well. He earned recognition, status, and pay increases. His aggressive, delinquent behaviors ceased and in the years since have not reappeared.

Whitman (1969) discusses a similar case in which treatment was successful with a narcissistic, exhibitionistic individual who was referred for therapy after being picked up by the police for exposing himself in the subway. During the course of his therapy he decided to convert his amateur golf status to a professional one, and he went on the circuit. He expressed the sublimation effect in his observation to the therapist: "When I am on the putting green holding my putter tightly (illustrated by patient grasping his hands before his groin) with the huge gallery watching every move I make with it, I feel I won't ever have to flash again."

Another striking example is the patient who came into treatment with me because of his concern about his fire-setting proclivities. Sublimation and reaction formation blended in his adaptive solution of then becoming a fireman.

In essence, then, approaches such as "topping" the patient, clarification, and confrontation, as well as the resource of group therapy, are what prove helpful in converting a character disorder into a more straightforward neurotic condition. The resistances of character disorders are comparatively unyielding, and repeated clarification and confrontation are necessary before the therapeutic work can get under way. Once that is accomplished, the more conventional procedures used in treating neurotic individuals can then be inaugurated.

10

Psychoanalysis and the Literary Arts

The bridge between psychoanalysis and the literary arts is wide and sturdy; it rests on four pillars: (1) therapeutic yield, (2) subject matter, (3) goals, and (4) prerequisite talents and disposition.

Overlapping Therapeutic Functions

Whereas poetry and the literary arts seek to illuminate, psychoanalysis seeks to unravel. Both address what Edmund Gosse, in a confidence to Henry James, referred to as the "obstinate twist" in the hidden personality. Art often, and psychoanalytic treatment more often, moves toward the achievement of that "quieter time" that Gosse, through writing, later reached: "Some beginnings of that Sophoclean period when the wild beast dies. He is not dead, but tamer; I understand him and the trick of his claws" (Hyde 1969, p. 89).

Edmund Wilson, at one point in the course of his monumental literary career, also experienced "a sort of a nervous breakdown." Later, when extending consolation to the poet Louise Bogan, another writer in psychic difficulties, he revealed the way out that he had found: "Give literary expression to your internal conflict and ranklings. . . . Once you get the experience out of your system in a satisfactory literary form, you can thumb your nose at the world." The processes of catharsis and, after catharsis, *mastery,* as both writer and analyst know, occur during literary creation as well as in psychotherapy. Each facilitates the experiencing of one's feelings and thoughts under the domain of one's self-regulatory capacities, the observing ego.

John Steinbeck, joining Edmund Gosse and Edmund Wilson, also felt that the writer is the only free man; he has but to write out his inner distress to gain emancipation. We might content ourselves with but three further examples, two contemporary and one classic. Philip Roth (1988) says of his *The Facts: A Novelist's Autobiography* that it originated in an "effort to repossess my life . . . to retrieve my vitality, to transform myself into myself" (after a depressive reaction following surgery, when he found himself on the brink of emotional and mental dissolution, suffering a disruption in concentration, focus, and health). He details:

There's my neighborhood and its impact on my life. There's
a rather extended portrait of college, and its effect on my
life. There's a portrait of a very lurid and tragic marriage,
and its impact on my life. There's a picture of a key scene in
my struggle with my Jewish critics, and its effect on my
life. . . . Pretty intimate revelations. It answered my curiosity about how it all had come to pass. And I wrote my way
out of a serious depression [p. 287]

The book presents us with raw chunks of emotion and
experience, the writing of which helped him to sort out
and to integrate — all in all, a psychotherapeutic exercise.

Another sensitive and aware report of how writing
can become a deeply therapeutic experience is offered by
Goldberg (1986):

I know this writing with my tired, resistant brain is the
deepest I'll get on the earth. Not the joy or ecstasy I feel
sometimes or the momentary flashes of enlightenment, but
this touching of the nitty-gritty of my everyday life and
standing in it and continuing to write is what breaks my
heart open so deeply to a tenderness . . . toward myself . . .
A glowing compassion for all . . . and it comes from me
naturally as I write and break down the hard, solid crusts of
thought in my own mind and the way I limit myself. [p. 136]

The third example: De Courcel (1988), in an enlight-
ening biography of Tolstoy, views his writing as an
expression of the "healing energies in his nature." Tolstoy, as he once said of Dostoyevsky, was himself also "a
man who was all struggle." Out of this struggle, both men
grew into writers who searched to decipher the meaning
of life, their own particularly, the works of each reflecting

their "continuous, unending struggle with their feelings" (p. 349).

Tolstoy discovered that he could use writing not merely to record and to deal with his inner conflicts, but to become, in each of his imagined characters, the many persons expressing themselves within him. Wilson (1988) shows how Tolstoy projected his own conflicts and experiences onto characters as disparate as Pierre, Nikolai Rostov, Levin, and Anna Karenina, herself. By the time Tolstoy had finished that novel, he had "gobbled up and used one large part of himself." Writing provided him with a means of ordering his chaotic inner life, of dealing with all the inconsistent roles (lecher, saint, husband, historian, dissident) that he liked to play. He recognized that it was Dickens and Sterne who had come to his rescue, showing him that in fiction he could master the shards of his selfhood and devise a coherence that he had been lacking.

An intriguing postscript to Wilson's work reveals that it eventually became more and more difficult for Tolstoy to integrate the disparate selves that he expressed in his creative work, to reconcile his intellectual rationalism with his passionate temperament. As his fiction dried up, he became, I would add, much like Oscar Wilde, Truman Capote, and Ernest Hemingway, "busy making a fictitious character out of himself."

An interesting piece of experimental evidence stands alongside the foregoing empirical tapestry. Kiecalt-Glaser and colleagues (Goleman 1989) conducted a study in which college students and other volunteers spent 20 minutes for four consecutive days writing about their most traumatic experiences and their feelings about them. The topics included the subjects' experiences of having been sexually abused, brushes with suicide, and family violence.

The investigators found that writing about these unsettling personal topics, which many of the subjects had never discussed with anyone, produced significant increases in the subjects' levels of T cells, the specialized immune cells which fight infection. Two important conclusions can be drawn from this study: (1) confronting traumatic memories (which is part of the process of psychotherapy) strengthens the immune system, the body's line of defense against bacteria, viruses, and cancer, and (2) writing can be one form of psychotherapy.

Shared Subject Matter

At the interface between novelist-playwright-poet and therapist is to be found common ground on which kindred spirits meet. Along with other shared elements, subject matter is often the same. As the analyst is allowed privileged entry into peoples' lives, so, too, is the writer, and through him the reader, into characters' lives. Then, as in a square dance, corners reverse. As patients bring to the analyst, the novelist brings to the reader, news of the human experience, news of the intimate sphere in which others live, from the inside of their marriages, their workplaces, their bedrooms, their heads and hearts and skins and secret selves — the stuff that heart-to-heart talks with even our best friends consistently leave us still wanting.

Michael Miller (1989), from his dual vantage point as writer and psychologist, states, "Before our times,

there were no sociological questionnaires [and we can add
clinical interviews] to document what we did to and with
one another. Instead, we turned to literature . . . to
explore the whole gamut of both tragic and comic . . . in
human relations." Thus we draw from, as well as share
the aim of, the novelist, who, as Henry James (Hyde
1969, p. 22) writes, "undertakes to tell tales and to report
with *truth on the human scene.*"

John Dunne (1989) notes, "The writer is always an
outsider, with his nose pressed against the window — on
the other side of which he finds his material." How many
analysts are similarly situated, and similarly motivated in
choosing our profession?

Our common terrain is defined by its depth and its
breadth; we stand together in our fascination with human
reality at its most complex and subtle. Anatole Broyard
(1989) speaks of the kind of scrutiny a writer brings to the
business of mining material from relationships. What a
writer "liked best of all, when with others, was to poke
around in your anxiety and give it form."[1]

---

[1]At times (Matranga 1988) the overlap between the focus of the analyst and
the writer extends to the modern comedian as well. Billy Crystal and Rob
Reiner, for example, move toward sharing with creative writer and analyst
both the process and the content. They share that which "goes very close to
the bone . . . etching characters that are close to reality and merely twisting
them slightly. . . . We love to get laughs but are more satisfied in moving an
audience. . . . There are a lot of comedians who make you laugh, you have
a good time, but there's nothing sticking to your ribs. You're not leaving with
anything that got inside and stayed with you," says Billy Crystal (p. 3).

Rob Reiner points out, "All the characters are me. If I have something
to say, it's going to come out through them" (p. 4).

Crystal further confides, "In order to get the personal things, you've
got to dig into yourself and search around, and that's not so much fun. . . .
It can make you think," and adds, as the analyst might, "It can make you
feel — think and feel all at the same time" (p. 6).

Common Goals

What Plato said in his *Republic* of philosophers is equally true of psychoanalysts (and some literary artists): "We consider no trivial issues but how a person would live."

The special affinity often felt between the psychoanalyst and the poet may rest on the fact that they share common goals. It is true that no single theory of the function of poetry will suffice; yet one of the ultimate ends of art is to humanize life—to absorb us in experiencing its fullness and richness. Similarly, one of the ends of psychoanalytic treatment is to enable the patient to get in touch with this richness, to experience a full immersion in existence.

In the shadowy area at the edge of consciousness lie our feelings, without which we can neither know nor be ourselves. Beyond the removal of symptoms, the goal of analysis is to help the patient's inner self to stretch, breathe, look about, and grow. Both poet and analyst share the intent of extending, respectively, the reader's and the patient's realities. Both value, and centrally engage in, a probing experience. Bernard Malamud (1971), the writer, asserts, "Art must interpret, or it is mindless." So, too, must psychoanalysis.

The poet seeks to recognize the universal in people. This goal, too, is shared by the analyst. At the same time the poet may chart the particular, the unique in a character. Similarly, the psychoanalyst strives to recognize in the patient those elements that are his alone.

Real writers—those who create serious rather than formula work—give us experience and after that, we hope, some deeper truths. Real therapists, too.

John Updike (1968) takes this further, saying of fiction, "Only truth is useful. Only truth can be built upon. Writers have nothing to deliver but the truth, the truth in its details and shadings" (p. 210). This, too, is the main and proper business of the analyst.

Milan Kundera (1981), in an interview with Philip Roth, describes the novelist's desire, in striking congruence with the psychoanalyst's, "to grasp [an understanding of] his protagonist from all sides and in the fullest possible completeness . . . combining everything into a unified whole" (p. 381). And his view of the novelist's goal is equally the psychoanalyst's: "to generate an extremely sharp light which suddenly reveals the essence of a character and sums up his life situation" (p. 383).

Like T.S. Eliot (Plimpton 1988), we analysts know that "each venture is a new beginning, a raid on the inarticulate" (p. 187). Isaac Bashevis Singer (1978) elaborates further when he speaks of the task of the artist as one of holding up the truth "then twisted about to show a new and unexpected view" (p. 24). Is this not exactly what we strive for with our patients?

In an engaging piece, "Write Till You Drop," Annie Dillard (1989) sees the writer's goal as one of bringing to the reader a sense of "life heightened and its deeper mysteries probed." She continues, "Can the writer isolate and vivify all in experience that most deeply connects with our intellects and our hearts? Can the writer renew our hopes?" We might ask, "Can the psychoanalyst?"

Moving us further into the very marrow of therapy, we note a statement by another writer. One of the universals of art, Joyce Cary has perspicaciously observed, is that it embodies a statement of a fact joined by a feeling about the fact. The therapist's statements should similarly aim toward the wedding of intellect and affect.

In a riveting paper, "Fiction, Moral Philosophy and Truth-Telling," Lynne McFall (1989) defines truth, from the vantage points of the philosopher and the fiction writer, as "messy, ambiguous, recalcitrant." This is exactly what the psychoanalyst finds it to be. The recalcitrance of truth is, after all, what resistance, and in turn resistance analysis, is all about.

Prerequisite Talents and Disposition

In his essay, "What is Art?" Leo Tolstoy wrote, "It is on the capacity of man to receive another man's expression of feeling and experience those feelings himself that the activity of art is based." The word *therapy* could as validly be substituted for *art,* for Tolstoy's observation catches the very essence of empathy. We might similarly substitute *therapy* for *art* in the statement by Norma Rosen, "I take the goal of art to be a 'refining' (in the sense of increased sensitivity — heightening and widening) of our perceptions and responses."

As we join ranks as seekers of psychological truths, if analysts look more deeply, novelists, playwrights, and poets look no less keenly, and are, arguably, more sensitive to the nuances, the wrinkles that flesh out personality.

Be that as it may, the analyst and writer equally seek to develop the same overlapping talents, to sense the exact tissue of relationships, to refine their powers of observation, and from fresh angles on the variety and vicissitudes of experience.

"A writer," Tobias Wolff (1989) writes, must be willing and able "to say that unspeakable thing whicheveryone else in the house is too coy, or too frightened, or too polite to say" (p. 73). The same is true of the therapist. Hemingway (Brodsky 1988) puts it more graphically: "The most essential gift for a good writer is a built-in shockproof shit detector" (p. 27). James Baldwin (Hall 1967) concurs, "If you're an artist . . . you see things others don't admit are there" (p. 31). This is exactly what analysts should see and help the patient to see as well.

The best novelists and psychoanalysts come to their calling gifted with what E. F. Benson (Houseman 1933) called a "gimlet eye," one that is capable of pinpointing even the most uncomfortable and evasive truths. They are possessed of a temperament that stands against self-deception and is relentlessly unsentimental, unyielding, and frank.

Pritchett (1988) says of Chekhov's writing, and of writing in general, "Good stories do not come straight from real experience but evolve from contemplating an essence of it" (p. 29). Psychoanalyst and writer share here, as elsewhere, the deeper orientation aiming to sense this core of human issues.

Storr (1989) extends the discussion to include science and contends that art and science stand shoulder to shoulder in addressing the impulse to master reality through mental activity: Both are "concerned with seeking order in complexity, and unity in diversity" (p. 309). So, too—as scientist and as artist—hopefully, is the psychoanalyst.

All in all, then, the analyst, like the writer, strives for the vision to see what others do not see and the courage to face and speak that vision. From these, the writer builds his craft and the analyst conducts his treatment.

In closing, we may distill from two proverbs a touch of inspiration, first for the analyst and then for his/her technique. For the analyst there is a Jewish saying, "A wise man hears one word—and understands two."

And for analytic interventions, there is another: "A learned man's question already contains half the answer."

References

Ahsen, A. (1968). *Basic Concepts in Eidetic Psychotherapy.*
New York: Brandon House.

_____ (1977). *Psycheye: Self-Analytic Consciousness.* New
York: Brandon House.

Aichorn, A. (1936). *Wayward Youth.* London: Putnam.

Angyal, A. (1965). *Neurosis and Treatment: A Holistic
Theory.* New York: Wiley.

Appelbaum, S. A. (1966). Speaking with the second
voice: evocativeness. *Journal of American Psychoanalytic
Association* 14:462–477.

_____ (1977). A psychoanalyst looks at gestalt therapy.
In *A Handbook of Gestalt Therapy,* ed. C. Hatcher
and P. Himelstein, pp. 753–778. New York:
Grune & Statton.

Arango, A. C. (1989). *Dirty Words: A Psychoanalytic Insight.* Northvale, NJ: Jason Aronson.

Arieti, S. (1966). *American Handbook of Psychiatry.* Vol. 3. New York: Basic Books.

———— (1976). *Creativity, The Magic Synthesis.* New York: Basic Books.

Arnheim, R. (1969). *Visual Thinking.* Berkeley: University of California Press.

Arnold, M. (1960). *Emotion and Personality.* 2 vols. New York: Columbia University Press.

Arnold, M., and Gasson, J. A. (1954). *The Human Person.* New York: Ronald Press.

Auden, W. H. (1977). In *Writers at Work: The Paris Review Interviews,* ed. G. Plimpton. New York: Viking.

Barron, F. (1963). *Creativity and Psychological Health.* New York: Van Nostrand.

Basescu, S. (1981). Anxieties in the analyst: an autobiographical account. In *The Human Dimension in Psychoanalytic Practice,* ed. K. A. Frank, New York: Grune & Stratton.

Bellak, L. (1953). In *Specialized Techniques in Psychotherapy,* ed. G. Bychowsky and J. L. Despert, pp. 114–131. New York: Basic Books.

Bergmann, M. (1965). Future of Psychoanalysis, National Psychological Association for Psychoanalysis, New York, March.

Blanck, G. (1969–1970). Crossroads in the technique of psychotherapy. *Psychoanalytic Review* 56:498–510.

Bogard, H. M. (1967). Psychotherapists' reactions to suicidal patients. *Professional Digest, New York Society of Clinical Psychologists* 2:6–9.

Boosler, E. (1988). "Punchline"—I don't get it. *New York Times,* November 12.

Brodsky, J. (1988). How to read a book. *New York Times Book Review,* June 12.

Brody, J. (1988). Personal health. *New York Times,* April 7.

Broyard, A. (1988). Squalor of freedom. *New York Times,* February 11.

_____ (1989). Writers beware writers. *New York Times Book Review,* May 21.

Brunner, J. (1966). *Studies in Cognitive Growth.* New York: Wiley.

Butler, J. (1962). On the naturalistic definition of variables: an analogue of clinical analysis. *Research in Psychotherapy* 2:178–205.

Calvino, I. (1988). *Six Memos for the Next Millennium.* Boston: Harvard University Press.

Carkhuff, R. R., and Berenson, B. G. (1967). *Beyond Counseling and Therapy.* New York: Holt, Rinehart and Winston.

Chessick, R. D. (1983). *How Psychotherapy Heals: The Process of Intensive Psychotherapy.* Northvale, NJ: Jason Aronson.

Choron, J. (1967) *Suicide and the meaning of life.* Paper presented at the New York Society of Clinical Psychologists Symposium *Suicide: Its Meaning and Implications,* New York, March 24.

Colby, K. M. (1951). *A Primer for Psychotherapists.* New York: Ronald Press.

Coles, R. (1980). Personal interview, June 25.

Cousins, N. (1979). *Anatomy of an Illness: The Healing Power of Humor.* New York: Random House.

Cox, M., and Theilgaard, A. (1986). *The Mutative Metaphor.* New York: Tavistock Publications.

Currie, C. (1986). *Visits.* New York: Simon and Shuster.

Darwin, C. (1872). *The Expression of Emotions in Man and Animals.* Chicago: University of Chicago Press, 1965.

Davison, G. (1980). Psychotherapy process. *Cognitive Therapy and Research* 6:269–306.

DeCourcel, M. (1988). *Tolstoy: Man and Work.* New York: Viking.

Deri, S. (1968). Interpretation and language. In *Use of Interpretation in Treatment,* ed. E. Hammer, pp. 141–147. New York: Grune & Stratton.

Deutsch, F. (1953). Instinctual drives and intersensory perceptions during the analytic procedure. In *Drives, Affects, Behavior,* vol. 1, ed. R. Loewenstein, pp. 174–201. New York: International Universities Press.

Devereux, G. (1941). Some criteria for the timing of confrontations and interpretations. *International Journal of Psycho-Analysis* 32:19–24.

Dillard, A. (1989). Write till you drop. *New York Times Book Review,* May 8.

Dunne, J. (1989). Today Show, NBC, Sept. 6.

Ehrenberg, D.B. (1989). *Playfulness in therapy.* Paper presented at the meeting of the American Psychological Association Convention, April. San Francisco.

Einstein, A. (1946). *Autobiographical Notes.* New Jersey: Princeton University Press.

Eissler, K. (1985). Notes on problems of technique in the psychoanalytic treatment of adolescents. *Psychoanalytic Study of the Child* 40:431–449.

Ekstein, R. (1959). Thoughts concerning the nature of the interpretive process. In *Readings in Psychoanalytic Psychology,* ed. M. Levitt, pp. 266–281. New York: Appleton-Century-Crofts.

Enright, J. B. (1972). Projection and play in therapy and growth. *Psychotherapy* 9:153–156.

Federn, P. (1952). *Ego Psychology and the Psychoses.* New York: Basic Books.

Fenichel, O. (1941). *Problems of Psychoanalytic Technique.* Albany, NY: Psychoanalytic Quarterly.

Fine, R. (1968). Interpretation: the patient's response. In *Use of Interpretation in Treatment,* ed. E. Hammer, pp. 110–120. New York: Grune & Stratton.

Fink, P. (1986). *Metaphor in Psychotherapy.* Paper delivered at Conference of the National Association of Poetry Therapy. New York City, June 6.

Fisher, K. A. (1966). Psychotherapy as play. *Arts and Sciences, New York University Bulletin* 66:28–33.

Freud, S. (1904). *The Psychoanalytic Method. Standard Edition* 6:341–480.

_____ (1905). Jokes and their relationship to the unconscious. *Standard Edition* 8:201–412.

_____ (1913). On beginning the treatment. *Standard Edition,* 13:411–422.

_____ (1933). *New Introductory Lectures on Psychoanalysis.* New York: W. W. Norton.

_____ (1937). Analysis terminable and interminable. *The Complete Psychological Works of Sigmund Freud,* vol. 23, pp. 209–254. London: Hogarth Press, 1974.

_____ (1949). *Civilization and Its Discontents.* New York: Basic Books.

_____ (1949). *Outline of Psychoanalysis.* New York: W. W. Norton.

_____ (1954). *The Origin of Psychoanalysis: Letters to Wilhelm Fliess: 1887–1902.* New York: Basic Books.

Fromm-Reichmann, F. (1950). *Principles of Intensive Psychotherapy.* Chicago: The University of Chicago Press.

Gallway, W. T. (1974). *The Inner Game of Tennis.* New York: Random House.

Gauther, S. (1968). Picasso: interview. *Look,* December 10, pp. 36–42.

Gendlin, E. T. (1981). *Focusing.* New York: Bantam.

Gendlin, E. T., and Olsen, L. (1970). The use of imagery in experiential focusing. *Psychotherapy: Theory, Research and Practice* 7:221–226.

Giovacchini, P. (1967). Transference, incorporation and synthesis. *International Journal of Psycho-Analysis* 48:61–67.

Glover, E. (1955). *The Technique of Psychoanalysis.* New York: International Universities Press.

Goldberg, N. (1986). *Writing Down the Bones.* Boston: Shambhala Publications.

Goldfarb, A. A., and Turner, H., II. (1958). Utilization and effectiveness of "brief therapy." *American Journal of Psychiatry* 109:792–799.

Goldstein, K. (1942). *Aftereffects of Brain Injuries in War.* New York: Grune & Stratton.

—— (1948). *Languages and Language Disturbances.* New York: Grune & Stratton.

—— (1963). *Human Nature in the Light of Psychopathology.* New York: Schocken.

Goleman, D. (1989). Researchers find that optimism helps the body's defense system. *New York Times,* April 20.

Gonzalez-Crussi, F. (1988). *On the Nature of Things Erotic.* New York: Viking.

Gorelick, K. (1989). Rapproachment between the arts and the psychotherapies. *The Arts in Psychotherapy* 16:149–155.

Graves, R. (1984). Genius. *Playboy,* May, pp. 82–85.

Greenberg, L., and Safran, J. (1989). Emotion in psychotherapy. *American Psychologist* 44:19–29.

Greenson, R. (1960). Empathy and its vicissitudes. *International Journal of Psycho-Analysis* 41:418–424.

—— (1971). The "real" relationship between the patient and the psychoanalyst. In *The Unconscious Today*, ed. M. Kanzer, pp. 213–232. New York: International Universities Press.

—— (1978). *Explorations in Psychoanalysis*. New York: International Universities Press.

Greenwald, H. (1967). Personal communication.

Gregory, B. (1924). *The Nature of Laughter*. London: Routledge and Kegan Paul.

Greif, A. (1985). Masochism in the therapist. *The Psychoanalytic Review* 72:491–501.

Gussow, M. (1988). *Caprice and Melancholy in Marriage*. New York: Plenum.

Hall, D. (1967). Speaking of books, a clear and simple style. *New York Times Book Review*, May 7.

Hammer, E. (1958). *The Clinical Application of Projective Drawings*. Springfield, IL: Charles C Thomas.

—— (1961). *Creativity*. New York: Random House.

—— (1964). Creativity and feminine ingredients in young male artists. *Perceptual and Motor Skills* 19:414.

—— (1965). President's column: of diagnosis, research, and the therapy hour. *New York Society of Clinical Psychologists Newsletter* 13:1–2.

—— (1966). Symptoms of sexual deviation: dynamics and etiology. *Psychoanalytic Review* 55:5–27.

—— (1968). *The Use of Interpretation in Treatment*. New York: Grune & Stratton.

—— (1978). Interpretations couched in the poetic style.

International Journal of Psychoanalytic Psychotherapy,
vol. 7, pp. 240–253. New York: Jason Aronson.
—— (1984). *Creativity, Talent and Personality.* Malabar,
FL: Krieger.

Havens, L. (1988). Sigmund the conqueror. *The New York
Times,* October 2.

Heckscher, P. (1987). *The Public Happiness.* New York:
Knopf.

Herma, H. (1968). The therapeutic act. In *Use of Interpretation in Treatment,* ed. E. Hammer, pp. 121–128.
New York: Grune & Stratton.

Hildebrand, A. (1933). *Problems of Form, Painting and
Sculpture.* New York: Julian.

Hollingshead, P., and Redlich, F. (1958). *Social Class and
Mental Illness.* New York: Wiley.

Holroyd, M. (1988). *Bernard Shaw.* Vol. 1. New York:
Random House.

Holt, G. (1983). *Free to be Good or Bad.* New York: Evans.

Housman, A. E. (1933). *The Name and Nature of Poetry.*
Cambridge, England: Cambridge University Press.

Howard, P. (1981). *Words Fail Me.* New York: Oxford
University Press.

Huxley, A. (1963). *Literature and Science.* New York:
Harper & Row.

Hyde, H. M. (1969). *Henry James at Home.* New York:
Farrar, Straus and Giroux.

Ionesco, E. (1964). *Writings on the Theatre.* New York:
Grove Press.

Jackson, J. H. (1926). *Eine Studie über Krämpfe.* Berlin: S.
Karger.

—— (1958). *Selected Writings.* Ed. J. Taylor. New York:
Wiley.

Jones, E. (1953). *The Life and Work of Sigmund Freud.* Vol.
1. New York: Basic Books.

Jong, E. (1988). Time has been kind to the nymphet:
"Lolita 30 years later." *New York Times Book Review,*
June 5, pp. 3, 46.

Justice, B. (1988). *Who Gets Sick.* New York: Tarcher.

Kanzer, M. (1958). Image formation during free association. *Psychoanalytic Quarterly* 27:465–468.

Kapecs, J. (1957). Observations on screens and barriers
in the mind. *Psychoanalytic Quarterly* 28:62–77.

Kenner, H. (1988). Review of *G. B. Shaw: Collected
Letters, 1911–1925. New York Times Book Review,*
September 25, p. 3.

Kepes, G. (1965). *The Nature of Motion.* New York:
George Braziller.

_____ (1966). *The Education of Vision.* New York: George
Braziller.

Kohut, H. (1978). Psychoanalysis in a troubled world. In
The Search for the Self, ed. P. Ornstein, pp. 245–263.
New York: International Universities Press.

Kris, E. (1950). On preconscious mental processes. *Psychoanalytic Quarterly* 19:540–560.

_____ (1951). Ego psychology and interpretation in psychoanalytic therapy. *Psychoanalytic Quarterly* 28:
62–77.

_____ (1952). *Psychoanalytic Explorations in Art.* New York:
International Universities Press.

Krueger, R. (1986). *The Last Taboo: Money as Symbol and
Reality in Psychotherapy and Psychoanalysis.* New York:
Brunner/Mazel.

Kubie, L. (1953). The concept of normality and neurosis.
In *Psychoanalysis and Social Work,* ed. M. Heimer, pp.

312–334. New York: International Universities Press.

———— (1961). Creativity and personality levels. In *Personality Dimensions of Creativity,* ed. E. Hammer, pp. 101–117. New York: Lincoln Institute for Psychotherapy.

Kundera, M. (1981). *Book of Laughter and Forgetting.* New York: Viking.

———— (1984). *The Unbearable Lightness of Being.* New York: Viking.

Laing, R. D. (1969). *The Politics of the Family.* Toronto: CBC.

Langs, R. J. (1976a). *The Bipersonal Field.* New York: Jason Aronson.

———— (1976b). The misalliance dimension in Freud's case histories. I: The case of Dora. *International Journal of Psychoanalytic Psychotherapy* 5:301–317.

———— (1976c). *The Therapeutic Interaction.* 2 vols. New York: Jason Aronson.

Levenson, E. (1985). *The Ambiguity of Change.* New York: Basic Books.

Levy, L. H. (1963). *Psychological Interpretation.* New York: Holt, Rinehart and Winston.

Loewald, E. (1960). On the therapeutic action of psychoanalysis. *International Journal of Psycho-Analysis* 41:16–33.

Loewenstein, R. M. (1957). Some thoughts on interpretation in the theory and practice of psychoanalysis. *Psychoanalytic Study of the Child* 7:308–324.

Luborsky, L., Chandler, M., Auerbach, A. H., et al. (1971). Factors influencing the outcome of psychotherapy: a review of quantitative research. *Psychological Bulletin* 75:145–185.

Malamud, B. (1971). Letter to the editor. *New York Times Book Review,* September 8.

_____ (1971). *The Tenants.* New York: Farrar, Straus and Giroux.

Marcuse, H. (1989). *One-Dimensional Man.* New York: Norton.

Maslow, A. (1957). *Emotional blocks to creativity.* Paper presented at Creative Engineering Seminars, US Army Engineers, Ft. Belvoir, VA, April 24.

Matranga, S. (1988). The buddy system. *The Cable Guide* 7:18–25.

McCarthy, M. (1988). *Hannah's Needs.* New York: Viking.

McFall, L. (1989). Fiction, moral philosophy, and truth telling. *Connections* 3:2–3.

Meng, H., and Freud, E. (1964). *Sigmund Freud and Oscar Pfister: Psychoanalysis and Faith.* New York: Basic Books.

Menninger, K. (1958). *Theory of Psychoanalytic Technique.* New York: Basic Books.

Merkin, D. (1988). *Enchantment.* New York: Scribner's.

Miller, M. (1989). Their cheatin' hearts. *New York Times Book Review,* January 29.

Mullahy, P. J. (1986). *Freud and the Rat Man.* New Haven, CT: Yale University Press.

Naumberg, M. (1955). Art as symbolic speech. *Journal of Aesthetic Art Criticism* 13:435–450.

Nelson, M. C. (1965). Paper presented at the meeting of the New York Society of Clinical Psychologists, *Second-Hand Patient,* New York, Jan. 4.

Nichols, L. (1968). Talk with John Updike. *New York Times,* April 7.

Nydes, J. (1965). Personal communication.

——— (1968). Interpretation and the therapeutic act. In *Use of Interpretation in Treatment,* ed. E. Hammer. New York: Grune & Stratton.

Oates, J. C. (1988). *The (Woman) Writer: Occasions and Opportunities.* New York: E. P. Dutton.

——— (1989). *American Appetites.* New York: E. P. Dutton.

Ornstein, A., and Ornstein, P. (1975). On the interpretive process in psychoanalysis. *International Journal of Psychoanalytic Psychotherapy* 4:219–271.

Padus, E. (1986). *Emotions and Health.* Emmaus, PA: Rodale.

Paivio, A. (1973). Psychophysiological correlates of imagery. In *The Psychophysiology of Thinking,* ed. F. McGuigan and R. Schoonover, pp. 263–295. New York: Academic.

Pezdek, K. (1985). The eyes have it. *American Health,* May, pp. 11–19.

Plimpton G. (1988). *Writers at Work.* New York: Penguin.

Prescott, O. (1970). Looking at books. *Look,* February 10, pp. 14–19.

Pritchett, V. S. (1988). Chekhov: a spirit set free. *New York Times,* October 7.

Rako, S., and Mazer, H. (eds.) (1983). *Semrad: The Heart of a Therapist.* New York: Jason Aronson.

Reik, T. (1948). *Listening with the Third Ear.* New York: Farrar, Straus and Giroux.

——— (1963). Personal communication.

Reyher, J. (1963). Free imagery: an uncovering procedure. *Journal of Clinical Psychology* 19:454–459.

Robertiello, R., Friedman, D., and Pollens, R. (1963). *The Analyst's Role.* New York: Citadel.

Rogers, C. (1970). *The Therapeutic Relationship and Its Impact.* New York: Wiley.

Roth, P. (1988). *The Facts: A Novelist's Autobiography.* New York: Norton.

Ruesch, J. (1961). *Therapeutic Communication.* New York: Norton.

Sands, S. (1984). The case for humor in psychotherapy. *Psychology Review* 71:441–460.

Sanville, J. (1987). Creativity and the construction of the self. *Psychoanalytic Review* 74:263–279.

Sarton, M. (1971). *Journal of a Solitude.* New York: W. W. Norton.

Schur, M. (1972). *Freud: Living and Dying.* New York: International Universities Press.

Seaver, E., ed. (1966). *Epitaphs of Our Times: The Letters of Edward Dahlberg.* New York: George Braziller.

Seidenberg, R. (1989). Review essay. *Psychoanalytic Psychology* 6:97–110.

Shaffer, L. (1947). The problem of psychotherapy. *American Psychologist* 2:389–392.

Sharpe, E. F. (1951). *Dream Analysis.* London: Hogarth Press.

Shaw, G. B. (1985). *Collected Letters, 1911–1925.* New York: Viking.

Sheikh, A. A. (1977). Editorial: mental images, ghosts of sensation? *Journal of Mental Imagery* 1:1–2.

Sheikh, A. A., and Panagiotous, N. (1975). Use of mental imagery in psychotherapy: a critical review. *Perceptual and Motor Skills* 41:555–585.

Singer, I. B. (1988). Interview. *New York Times Book Review,* July 28.

Singer, J. (1974). *Imagery and Daydream Methods in Psychotherapy and Behavior Modification.* New York: Academic Press.

Storr, A. (1989). *Churchill's Black Dog, Kafka's Mice.* New York: Grove.

Strachey, J. (1934). The nature of the therapeutic action of psycho-analysis. *International Journal of Psycho-Analysis* 15:127–159.

Strupp, H. H. (1989). Psychotherapy: can the practitioner learn from the researcher? *American Psychologist* 44:717–724.

Sullivan, H. S. (1947). *Conceptions of Modern Psychiatry.* Washington, DC: Wm. A. White Psychiatric Foundation.

Timms, E., and Segal, N. (1988). *Freud in Exile.* New Haven: Yale University Press.

Tirnauer, L. (1967). Notes for a happy psychotherapy. *Voices* 3:63–64.

Tomalin, C. (1988). *A Secret Life.* New York: Knopf.

Updike, J. (1968). Interview. *New York Times Book Review,* April 7, pp. 9–11.

—— (1977). On poetry. *New York Times Book Review,* April 10, p. 3.

Warren, M. (1961). Significance of the visual images during the analytic session. *Journal of American Psychoanalysis Association* 9:504–518.

Wellness Letter (1988). A good medicine. October. Berkeley: University of California Press.

West, P. (1988) Purple Prose, *New York Times Book Review,* April 17, p. 10.

Wexler, D. A. (1974). A cognitive theory of experiencing self-actualization and therapeutic process. In *Innovations in Client-Centered Therapy,* ed. D. A. Wexler and L. N. Rice, pp. 49–116. New York: Wiley.

Wexler, F. (1969). The antiachiever. *Psychoanalytic Review* 56:461–467.

Whitman, R. M. (1969). Psychoanalytic speculations about play: tennis—the duel. *Psychoanalytic Review* 56:197–214.

Wilson, R. (1988). *Tolstoy.* New York: Viking.

Wolf, V. (1973). *On Writing.* New York: Random House.

Wolff, T. (1989). *Matters of Life and Death.* New York: Atlantic Monthly Press.

Wolk, R. L. (1967). The Kernal interview. *Journal of Long Island Consultation Center* 5:41–51.

Yalom, I. (1980). *Existential Psychotherapy.* New York: Basic Books.

Zikmund, V. (1975). Physiological correlates of visual imagery. In *The Function and Nature of Imagery,* ed. P. Sheeham, pp. 355–387. New York: Academic Press.

Index

Words, patient's need of, 92–93   Yalom, I., 67–68
Wordsworth, William, 16
Writings on the Theatre (Ionesco), 17   Zikmund, V., 59